Making Sense of Things
Towards a Theology of
Homegrown Christian Education

MAKING SENSE OF THINGS

Towards a Theology of
Homegrown Christian Education

David W. Perry, editor

THE SEABURY PRESS · NEW YORK

1981
The Seabury Press
815 Second Avenue
New York, N.Y. 10017

Printed in the United States of America

Library of Congress Cataloging in Publication Data
Main entry under title:

Making sense of things.

   1. Christian education (Theology)   I. Perry, David W.
BV1464.M34   207   80-26005
ISBN 0-8164-2297-4

Contents

The Authors

J. KENNETH ASEL, rector of St. Michael's Church in Pinneville, Louisiana, has been a regional religious education coordinator (RREC), in Province IV since 1978.

WILLIAM P. BAXTER, JR., rector of St. Thomas' Church in Owings Mills, Maryland, was program director for the diocese of South Carolina and a RREC in Province IV.

TED L. BLUMENSTEIN, rector of St. Paul's Church in Marion, Ohio, is a RREC in Province V and has had much experience in youth ministries and leadership training.

RICHARD A. BOWER, associate rector of Trinity Church in Princeton, New Jersey, has written and published music for the liturgies of The Book of Common Prayer. He is a RREC in Province II.

FRIEDA CARNELL, who was formerly a RREC in Province II, is now president of the ECW (Episcopal Church Women) in the diocese of Albany, a college administrator, and a graduate student at the State University of New York (SUNY).

DOUGLAS T. COOKE, a diocesan staff person in Connecticut, is involved with a variety of programs in Christian education. He was formerly a RREC in Province I.

SYLVAN HEATH, **RREC** in Province I at present, is also parish education consultant for the diocese of Rhode Island and coordinator of the national Christian Education Research Project.

ELIZABETH B. HIGH, **RREC** in the South/Central area of Province VII, is also missioner for education and leadership training in the diocese of Long Island.

JACK HILYARD, a **RREC** in Province VIII, is a Christian education staff person in the diocese of Oregon and co-author of *Becoming Family* (St. Mary's Press), a resource book in intergenerational education.

FRED J. HOWARD, associate coordinator for religious education of the Episcopal Church, has held a number of Christian education posts in Province VII and in the diocese of Northwest Texas.

WILLIAM F. KIRKPATRICK, a **RREC** in Province II, is assistant to the bishop of Rochester for education, planning, and mutual ministry, and a consultant in the areas of parish life, spiritual renewal, and faith development.

THOMAS J. MCELLIGOTT, who is **RREC** in Province VI, has been involved in many phases of Christian education since 1945.

NORMA MARRS, a **RREC** in Province VII, has worked as a religious educator in a number of dioceses and parishes.

JAMES H. OTTLEY, who is executive secretary for Province IX, also serves as director of the Episcopal University Center and Hot-Line in Panama City, Panama.

DAVID W. PERRY, national coordinator for religious education of the Episcopal Church, is editor of *Home Grown Christian Education* (The Seabury Press, 1979) and coeditor of *Aware*.

NANCY RAYFIELD, education officer of the diocese of Indianapolis and RREC in Province V, is also an artist, designer, and potter.

DOROTHY M. WATT, RREC in Province III, has wide experience in Christian education on the diocesan and parish levels.

LADONNA M. WIND, RREC in Province VII, is involved, on the diocesan level, as a youth enabler, program developer, and communications person, and is a parish consultant in youth ministry.

Making Sense of Things
Towards a Theology of
Homegrown Christian Education

Introduction

DAVID W. PERRY

Theology is a word that frightens many people for a variety of reasons. In some people's minds, theology is inextricably linked with dogma—something one is told one *must* believe. This was brought home to me quite clearly while conducting a teacher training session. A newly-recruited Christian educator was seated at my right and had been eying me rather suspiciously during my presentation on the creeds of the church. When I had finished talking I wasn't at all surprised to see him raise his hand.

"I don't know about all of this," he said, "I don't know about 'theology' or 'incarnation' or 'virgin birth.' I just go to church. Theology is for you priests. Just tell me how to keep my class of 8th grade boys from destroying themselves or the guild room and I'll be happy!"

This isn't at all an unusual response—the perception of theology as a sort of trade secret of priests and of little practical use to laypersons involved in the world and in day-to-day living. And there are few persons involved in Christian education who have not had to reassure or counsel a distracted Christian-educator-to-be who decides to leave the whole program because he or she cannot accept some point of dogmatic theology subscribed to by the church, and therefore feels unable to go on to teach the Christian young, who must surely be brought to terms with the basic tenets of theology.

Many people do indeed view theology as strictly in the realm of seminaries, priests, and rather elite, other-worldly thinkers. Of course, this attitude is nurtured in part by the deadly, jargon-ridden language in which most theology until very recent times has been written. And, more importantly, it has to do with a misunderstanding on the part of many believing people about what theology really is. The fact is that the words *theology* and *dogma* (and *boring*) are not inextricably linked at all. Many people have perfectly workable and sound theologies and don't even know they have them!

Theology simply means *thinking about God.* A person who seeks to understand God and live in his presence is possessed of a growing or developing theology. Despite all of the learned tomes, theology is not so much a matter of the head as it is born out of life.

To speak theologically is to reflect on our experiences of God. To speak theologically is to look at our experiences of life and put the pieces together into a mosaic picture of our real involvement with God. We create a theology when we try to express what we "see" when we look at our life and our being in its totality. Theology is an attempt to make sense out of action—out of the things we do and the things that are done to us. The creeds professed by most Christians are themselves statements which grew out of people trying to make sense of their experience with the Risen Christ in the Power of the Spirit.

There are many different ways of perceiving theology. For me, theological reflection is a process. I see theology as a reflection about life and life is always changing, renewing, and forming. My theological reflection is not accidental—it is an intentional act or series of acts in which I consciously think about and name the moments of life and experiences of God. My theological process involves knowing, naming, and telling the story—and stories—that have meaning for me. And it is in the process of making meaning of the events of life that I come to tell my story and have a theology. Theology is a way of living the story.

And of course my story is really our story, the story of the human family of God. My experience must always be in terms of and in the context of other human beings, and in the spirit of God's creation. We are members of the same Body. Our theologies, if they are true and real, must be alive as life itself—in the moments of hurt and in healing, in the midst of despair, and in elation. I can form my theology and understand my story because of our shared existence in the human family, our shared life in the Body.

My story finds its roots in the story of the people of God as it is recorded in scripture, in history, and in the traditions of the church itself. In this rich fabric I find threads which are the *real* color of my life. The truth of those images and symbols is verified by my experience in the Christian community.

"Jesus loves me this I know, for the Bible tells me so," is, for me, only a partially true statement. The Bible, as the story of God's people in response to his call, is true for me because the stories it tells are stories I have found to be true in my own life. I *know* the Resurrection is true, not because the Bible and the creeds tell me it is, but because in my own living I have seen hope and life and eternity born out of the rocky tomb of despair. I have known an Easter morning. The Bible is true because we find that truth in our lives and in our community.

My theology is one that does not flourish in private.

By sharing it in the community, I gain in understanding and am able to live what I know to be true. And this act of sharing gives me the opportunity to encourage and enable other people to grow in their awareness of God's presence and call.

Real theology is at the root of our actions and grows from them. It is in the dynamics of action and in reflection on it that we find meaning and learn to grow. As Christians we *live theologically,* and this means that the process is unending—we move on to act more faithfully and to educate and to learn and grow accordingly ourselves.

Each person's story is a story that belongs to us all. To know and tell our stories is to rehearse and retell the acts of the human family as the people of God. And when we do this, we are empowered to continue acting faithfully as God's people.

Remember the story of Abram and Sarah? In telling that famous Biblical story today we can still experience what they experienced centuries ago: the fearfulness of setting out on a pilgrimage into the unknown; the uncertainties, the anxieties:

> The Lord said to Abram, 'Leave your own country, your kinsmen, and your father's house, and go to a country that I will show you.
>
> *Genesis 12:1*

And the Lord did not make the path of Abram and Sarah all that easy or reassuring, despite the grandeur of the promise of the journey. But God sustained them through all their trials. And we, too, have found and continue to find the sustaining presence of God on our journey to a far and unknown country. We know the story of Sarah and Abram is true because we have been with them on their journey as members of the same human family. And that knowing is a building block in the structure of our theology. But we know because *we know*, because *we experience*—not because we are *told* it is true.

In recalling the life and ministry and story of Martin Luther King, Jr., we can begin focus on the meaning of God's power in a broken world. And the understanding we gain from the facts of his life and what they mean help us form a theology for our lives and work:

> Like anybody, I would like to live a long life. Longevity has its place. But I'm not concerned about that now. I just want to do God's will . . . I've looked over and I've seen the promised land. I may not get there with you, but I want you to know . . . that we as a people will get to the promised land.

> I Believe that unarmed truth and unconditional love will have the final word in reality. That is why right, temporarily defeated, is stronger than evil triumphant.
>
> *Martin Luther King, Jr.*

Our theology informs our actions on our journey for justice and love. Many of us remember King's journey, and we took it with him.

The journey of boat people from Southeast Asia, from Haiti, from Cuba into the midst of the United States, into the heart of American life gives us an immediate insight into the fears, the perils, and the bravery of a pilgrim people on the move. And their experience, our shared experience with them, allows us to examine our thoughts about caring and hospitality and enables us to come to a new theology of welcome. Our actions and reflections on them can call us to review, to focus, to clarify our theologies.

When we deal with the "how" questions of ministry, we must also ask the "why" questions of theology. As

Christian educators, we must all reflect on our *actions*—
past, present, and those anticipated in the future. Our
theology must be reflected in our lives, in our continuing journeys and development, and in our lifework of
building a faithful community.

These essays are the work of a group of active, dedicated Christian educators, religious education coordinators of the Episcopal Church. They are the stories and
signs and symbols and images of searchers and pilgrims
who are seeking to make meaning of life. They are
theologies: theological affirmations trying to make sense
of the intricate and shared life of the Christian family.

1

Transcendant Vs. Measurable

by J. KENNETH ASEL

Education in the church is often bad. Even more often, it is an afterthought. Churches that claim to take their educational ministries seriously are likely to do so by equating religious facts with education, and then proceed to shovel as many items of information into their students as possible. In the Episcopal Church, we usually avoid that problem by retreating to our beautiful and historic liturgy, and proclaiming that all true Christians will eventually see its wonder and respond in faith.

Strong words. But unfortunately, these strong words are only slightly, if at all, exaggerated. I would contend that our approach to Christian education is flawed in most instances because we fail to understand the dynamics of *voluntary* education. Most education programs tend to fall between two poles. Those emphasizing traditional schooling methods attempt to reproduce a public school atmosphere around the subject of religion. That situation will never work, primarily because churches are unable to enforce the negative sanction, such as poor grades and refusal of promotion, that are so important for many students. Better teacher training and the use of a more highly skilled teaching staff will not provide these sanctions. On the other extreme is the "unstructured" education program. This style emphasizes feelings and emotions. It makes, by necessity, every class an individual unit so that no child is confused after a protracted absence. By reducing education to its lowest common denominator, it shrinks to insignificance the level of commitment required for participation. Cheap Sunday School is of no more value than cheap grace.

The trick, of course, is to provide a vital, on-going experience that enlightens the student's intellect and enables him to transfer the wonder of the believer's encounter with his God into every aspect of his life. Thomas Groome of Catholic University of America says the same thing from another perspective. He writes, "Our Christian Education should help people to personally appropriate the meaning of their faith in a way which enables them to go on reinterpreting and doing its meaning in later life situations. In other words, our Christian education must enable people to become decision-makers who exercise their freedom as God's children in creating with him and with each other their future." ("Shared Christian Praxis") It is that connection between the intellect and experience, between the transcendant and the measurable, that brings people back. What takes place in their local Christian community on Sunday school is of no more value than cheap grace.

David Perry of the Episcopal Church Center has also written about the necessity of relating the transcendant and the measurable. "We have failed to open minds and hearts for visions of God. We have taught a static, stone vision of God which too often comes from someone else's experience/vision of God, rather than helping each person to discover the vital reality in his/her very own world . . . Christian education at its best, I believe, can find its focus in the life and witness of the whole Christian Community." ("Journeying Environment: A Theological Affirmation," *Aware,* vol III, no. 1)

The problems of realizing the educational ministry of the church are compounded by the seeming conflict between the transcendant and the measurable. It is extremely difficult to communicate a religion based on saga, story, and imagination to a highly technological age that not only doubts the existence of the transcendant, but would deny its importance even if it did exist. The scientific advances of the twentieth century are not anti-religious, but they are based on a set of principles that assume different things than religion. Biblical fundamentalists betray a profound misunderstanding of Scripture when they attempt to use it as a scientific textbook, resolving questions unimagined by its authors. The study of religion is a humanity. It is best understood in the context of its sister disciplines in the humanities—art, music, history, and literature. Verna Dozier describes the process of faith development as "the creation of an atmosphere in which the movement of the Holy can be responded to." ("Toward a Theology of Christian Education") A major task before religious educators is the development of systems to help humans become humane in an increasingly artificial environment.

Technology is not the only complication in contemporary religious education. Since the 1950's, minority groups have been successful in making demands upon the dominant society for recognition. Our social structure has resisted these demands. Surely racism is a part of this resistance, but an often overlooked aspect of resistance is that our economy and national myths are not prepared for these multi-ethnic demands. The concept of catholicity, so much of our faith in name, has much to address this issue. It was resolved, officially at least, very long ago that all people share essential equality before God. If that fundamental myth of our faith is to be a reality in the world, the church can provide leadership to that end.

So what should be done in parish education? Gabriel Moran defines Christianity as "an invitation to human intelligence and freedom to re-create the world." (*Design for Religion*) The key element in any educational process, he continues, is the presence of community. On a parish level, Moran seems to be saying that our intelligence needs to be informed of the great acts of redemption. Our human freedom must be inclined toward the will of God. The sagas of past generations are valuable in helping us discern the way God operates among his people. There is no "moral" to Christianity. There *is* a process, a methodology God uses in responding to his creation. The church's task is to learn that methodology in order to apply it to our own situation and to the future. It matters little that Christ rose from the dead, unless that Resurrection supplies hope for the hopeless. We are a chosen people. We are a people chosen for *service,* not privilege. Education in the church best fulfills its function when it finds in the Christian experience elements of service compelling enough to be performed again and again in the lives of new generations—until the Kingdom comes.

2

In God's Time

by WILLIAM BAXTER

My first observation about the ministry of Christian nurture is that this action is rooted in time, set in the give and take of God's graceful reaching out to his creatures and their response to this gift of grace and love. Upon reflection, I find that my notion of time is summed up for me in a book. This book is *The Shape of the Liturgy* by Dom Gregory Dix, and when I was in seminary we were told that we must read the chapter entitled, "The Sanctification of Time." What Dix set down in this lengthy chapter has profoundly shaped my understanding of the Christian view of time.

The topic of the chapter is the fundamental changes which occurred in the entire ethos of Christian life and worship during the fourth century. In the short space of 100 years from the accession of Constantine in AD 312 to the turn of the century, just before the sack of Rome by the Goths in AD 410, the Christian church experienced two fundamental changes which have come down from that day to this: First, with the embrace of Christianity by the Emperor Constantine, the church would henceforth be living and worshipping no longer in a hostile, but in a nominally Christian world. Secondly, as a result of this, the church came gradually to feel at home in the world, and so she became reconciled to *time*. The eschatological emphasis inevitably faded to be replaced by a sense of historical process. Not only the historical facts of God's saving act in Christ, but also an historical process which lay in wait down the years—a mission and work which stretched put into "God's time," nurtured by the regular representation of God's salvation in the Eucharistic feast. The results of these two changes for the life of the church cannot be overstated, for, quite simply they changed the whole of Christian understanding and life—and, thus, the title which Dix chose for this chapter on the fourth century is indeed apt: "The Sanctification of Time."

I believe that in our vision of Christian education we are direct inheritors of those fundamental events which occurred in the fourth century. To draw upon Dix once more and put it most plainly: "While the world hungered for martyrs, the church had trained men and women for Christian dying, since that was what the clash of the circumstances of history with the truth of the Gospel then demanded. . . . When the need of the new Christian world was for daily holiness, she trained men and women no longer for Christian *dying*, but for Christian *living*." And that has made all the difference and we stand in direct line of that inheritance. The point I would make in all of this is that the ministry of education has not always been with us nor made of whole cloth—this notion of the raising up and nurture of men and women for Christian living is rooted in an historical context and developed in the creative clash of Christian vision and common experience. If nothing else, Christian education is rooted in God's time.

In the field of Christian education, I know of no more troubling and divisive debate going on than that which centers upon the self-understanding of Christian educators themselves and their vision of their task and ministry. Throughout the Episcopal Church, and among our brothers and sisters in other traditions, there seem to be two ways of looking at religious education. One position sees the job of the educator as engaging the student in such a way as to pass on the heritage and faith which has in turn been passed down to us all. This process not only involves a learning faith, but would include the transmission of values, liturgies, and perceptions of the world. This is what John Westerhoff has called "enculturation" and it is a gradual, timely process. The other position sees the role of the church educator to be that of a willing participant in a confrontive experience for the learner. Christian education in this view provides the context whereby the learner is confronted by God's Spirit through his Word—given and received in faith. The result is that the learner is confronted by God's active and redeeming claim on his or her life and responds to this claim in concrete terms. Both of these views of the role and purpose of Christian education are voiced by many people from one end of the Episcopal Church to another—and beyond. To put it most plainly, the debate is *Nurture vs Conversion*. These two words perhaps draw the line most clearly. Is the essence of our ministry nurture, or conversion?

This debate seems to be a useless exercise in futility, and one which often drains our energy and takes our eyes off more pressing matters at hand. To debate over whether Christian education is most importantly *conversion* or *nurture* is to be led into a labyrinth of half-truth and overemphasis. I am convinced that the fullness of our ministry incorporates *both* of these aspects of the faith. I hope and pray that all of us might move beyond this kind of jousting and begin to confront what I feel is the more serious and profound challenge facing those involved in Christian education in our time. I believe that we must confront and face squarely, in an increasingly secular and nominally Christian world, the issue of integrity in what we do.

To me, the issue of integrity is a challenge to religious education in the church. My dictionary defines this word as: "the quality or state of being of sound moral principle; uprightness, honesty, and sincerity." Both the definition and ring of this word carry for me a challenge, as a world which increasingly does not believe looks at the church to see what it is we do for our children, for our young people, and for ourselves as adult Christians. The nature of this challenge is diverse, but let me try to suggest some of the issues before us.

· Does our behavior suggest integrity? Do we in our congregations and our opportunities for learning treat people as valuable children of God—or do we fool them by fast words and trendy whims? Do we promise what we have no intention of producing?

· Former Attorney General John Mitchell, in palmier days, suggested to a reporter, "Watch what we do, not what we say," and, unfortunately for him, some people did just that. But the same suggestion could apply to our programs and the question is, how would they stack up with what we promise and say about them?

· One of the beauties of the Anglican way is our use of doctrinal formulations to convey the mystery and grace of divine purpose in Creation. Do we use these formulations as intended or do we hide behind them and use them as defenses?

· Does the effect of our office and ministry further the freedom of God's people, or does it lead into the bondage of mindless adherence, that "escape from freedom" which Erich Fromm so aptly defines, in his book

of the same name, or do we instill such compliant behavior as to quench the human search for that which is
true and lasting? We can see the extreme results of this
in the bodies of Jonestown, a sad mixture of pernicious
evil and pitiful allegiance to an empty dream. But closer
to home, this issue offers much to ponder. For there is
a thin line between bondage on the one hand and the
kind of easy going commitment which is characterized
in New Yorker cartoons of contemporary Christians—
mannerly, inoffensive, and scarcely committed to anything. The vision which we offer is, in part, the fruit by
which we are known.

· Do we as leaders take the concept of "mutual ministry"
seriously enough? Can we face up to our absolute de-
pendence upon God's sustaining spirit and grace in our
lives? Can we share the ministry to God's people *with*
God's people and banish the specter of "triumphalism"
which has plagued us since we left the catacombs. Is the
Christian community where we live and worship—truly
a pilgrim band of seekers—signed and marked with a
cross and open to the wind of the Spirit?

· Along the same line, do we as educators show forth
Christ to a world so badly in need of him. The tempta-
tion toward cynicism and snobbish elitism is a constant
danger for those of us who lead—much like the asser-
tion that the hardest place to have a meaningful experience of worship is in front of the altar when you are
leading it. The danger is that we might come too close
to the mystery—it becomes tamed and named, and we
are left empty. Are we convicted of Christ? Do we live
in him as sinners and yet forgiven and loved beyond
measure? It is here that we have much to learn from the
charismatic renewal movement within and without our
church—for its very existence and vitality is a witness to

the emptiness of many pilgrim folk. I am convinced that we ignore the witness of these movements at our own peril.

· Church educators have the opportunity to aid Christians in coming to terms with momentous changes in life-style and vision in the next generation. But in approaching this task have we, as educators, sought God's will and guidance in personal life and witness? Do we in our own lifestyle have the serious Christian searching which we recommend for others?

· Many of us in our program planning and teaching aim at providing experiences which will lead people to become involved in God's struggle for human liberation and freedom. But have we done our homework, have we taken seriously the complexities and harsh realities of a world where many answers are not clearcut, where choices of personal and social witness are ambiguous? In a word, I believe that church educators must be as cautious about proclaiming mindless and uninformed Marxism and socialism as we have been about proclaiming civil religion and capitalism.

· I do not want you to be misled on this last point and hope that I do not sound too conservative; for I deeply believe that we should be in the business of "changed lives" and that one of the results of good religious education is strong and vibrant work and witness in God's world. However, I am often reminded of the last lines written by Kenneth Clark in his work entitled *Civilization*. Speaking of the future prospects for a strong and creative culture in the West, Clark says something like this: "With the moral and intellectual failure of Marxism, there is nothing left on the scene but heroic materialism—and that is not enough." I take Sir Kenneth's observations quite seriously and am troubled by the critique they contain of the prospects for great contributions from Christendom in the years ahead, but I am also dismayed when I see some church educators using as their philosophical base a simplistic and slightly "baptized Marxism" which would be rejected out of hand by serious social critics and conservative thinkers alike.

The issue for an increasingly unbelieving world is the integrity of the church as we go about our business and it is questions like these which make up the challenge. These are profound issues which go far beyond *nurture vs conversion,* and they will continue to face us as we move into the future. The answers lie not in policy and doctrine. The answers to the challenge lie in the ministry of each one of us as we are faced with day to day decisions of leading and equipping and even following the pilgrimage of God's people.

I have tried to suggest that we should see our ministry within the context of time and the events of God and man. Further, I have suggested what I see to be the decade ahead—the challenge of integrity in what we do for ourselves and others.

But lest we be too neat and tidy about all of this, I would remind all of us that whatever we do, in whatever circumstances, especially in the church, our ministry is difficult at best. Having seen ministry and education from the perspective of parish, diocese, and province, I know that the multitude of things which take our time and weigh upon our energy leave us precious little to think profound thoughts of ministry, of saving grace, of Christian work and witness in a lost and broken world. For those of you who feel like this, I would like to offer another way to look at what we do and a vision of its place and importance. I want to share three parables written by Sister Patricia Rooks, a fellow pilgrim. They speak of the task of religious education and our role and place in it.

1

I took a little child's hand in mine. He and I were to walk together for a while. I was to lead him to the Father. It was a task that overcame me, so awful was the responsibility. And so I talked to the child only of the Father. I painted the sternness of his face were the child to do something that would appease the Father's wrath. We walked under the tall trees. I said the Father had the power to send them crashing down, struck by his thunderbolts. We walked in the sunshine. I told of the greatness of the Father who made the burning, blazing sun. And one twilight we met the Father. The child hid behind me; he was afraid. He would not take the Father's hand. I was between the child and the Father. I wondered; I had been so conscientious, so serious.

2

I took a little child's hand in mine. I was to lead him to the Father. I felt burdened with a multiplicity of the things I had to teach him. We did not ramble, we hastened from one spot to another. At one moment we compared the leaves of the different trees. In the next moment we were examining a bird's nest. While the child was questioning me about the nest, I hurried him away to chase a butterfly. Did he chance to fall asleep I awakened him, lest he miss something I wished him to see. We spoke of the Father. Oh yes, often and rapidly I poured into his ears all the stories he ought to know, but we were interrupted often by the wind blowing, whose source we must trace. And then in the twilight we met the Father. The child merely glanced at him and then his gaze wandered in a dozen directions. The Father stretched out his hand; the child was not interested enough to take it. Feverish spots burned in his cheeks. He dropped exhausted to the ground and fell asleep. Again I was between the child and the Father. I wondered; I had taught him so many things.

3

I took a little child's hand to lead him to the Father. My heart was full of gratitude for the glad privilege. We walked slowly. I suited my steps to the short steps of the child. We spoke of the things the child noticed. Sometimes we picked the Father's flowers and stroked their soft petals and loved their bright colors. Sometimes it was one of the Father's birds. We watched it build its nest. We saw the eggs that were laid. We wondered, elated, at the care it gave its young. Often we told stories of the Father. I told them to the child and the child told them again to me. We told them, the child and I, over and over again. Sometimes we stopped to rest, leaning against one of the Father's trees, and letting his air cool our brows, and never speaking. And then in the twilight, we met the Father. The child's eyes shone. He looked lovingly, trustingly, eagerly up to the Father's face. He put his hand into the Father's hand. I was, for the moment, forgotten. I was content.

Which is your story?

One way to describe our calling is to say that we are to lead each other to the Father. The question raised here is where do you and I find ourselves in the parables. We can be so overwhelmed by the task of leading others that we hurry or we frighten—on the other hand, we can accept the task with some humility and grace and try our best in the only way we know to meet the Father and lead others to meet him too.

In the end, when all is said and done, the most important thing for us as teachers and leaders to realize is that *we are what we are:* simple, fragile children of God trying to get home and on our journey, trying to reach out to some others who are children, too, to bring them and ourselves to the Father. We all need to learn and grow and work to teach and lead more effectively, but in the end, it is only God's grace which carries us on.

3

Benchmarks for Christian Educators

by TED L. BLUMENSTEIN

The purpose of this paper is to set forth some theological statements that can be used by Christian educators as benchmarks when they are planning and evaluating programs.

An important underlying assumption is that everything any person or group of persons does communicates *something*. We are teaching by example at all times whether we intend to or not. Perhaps the first question we should ask ourselves at the outset of any program is, "What have I been teaching by my own conduct or lifestyle? Is this consistent with what I am seeking to do or to accomplish?"

The following principles are an attempt to set forth a description of "what I am seeking to do" through the activities that I can designate as "Christian education."

· *Programs Should Be Based on, and Reflective of, Theology Which Is in Accord with the Biblical and Theological Tradition of our Church*

The call of Abraham to move out in faith establishes a standard of risk taking for the people of God. Our Biblical heritage is one of openness, curiosity, and imagination. It does not offer easy answers or right answers.

It helps us to test and to live in tension. Jesus taught in parables in which a question is often answered with another question.

Our Anglican tradition sets forth three bases of faith: scripture, tradition, and reason. In accepting these we accept a life in the faith that is marked by constant searching, tension, conflict, and growth.

· *Everything We Do Ought To Contribute to and Be Supportive of the Total Life and Ministry of the Whole Church*

The Episcopal Church is an interdependent family that has both an organized and a dispersed "in the world" membership. We share a diverse set of ministries, all of which witness to the Lordship of Christ.

Congregational, diocesan, provincial, and national institutions need not be in competition. Each reinforces the other in the building up of the Body of Christ. The same is true, of course, of all "program areas," such as social action, evangelism, youth work, or lay ministry. People should be assisted in making the connections and seeing the essential oneness of the church.

· *Programs Should Include Both Understanding the Faith and Response to the Faith in Ethical Action*

The content of the faith needs to be taught in a way that enriches life by increasing our understanding of ourselves, our life together, and our God. However, no program, no matter how inspiring theologically, is complete unless a call to action is heard and acted upon. Therefore, there should be an impetus for creative response built into every educational event. The skills necessary for implementing our response are also an appropriate arena for Christian education efforts.

· *The Affirmation of Individuals and the Concern for their Growth Are of Primary Importance*

The total program environment should contribute to the affirmation of individuals: the content, the method, the setting, the leadership style, and the group life. This principle indicates a person-centered rather than a content-centered curriculum. In our concern for the whole person, we must have respect for the feelings, attitudes, and skills of persons as well as for their intellects. Educators and psychologists have described the developmental stages of persons and the educational tasks that are possible and profitable at the various stages. We need to apply this knowledge appropriately.

Every event or program should involve both leaders and participants in every phase of the planning and implementation. The personal integrity and creative ability of each person should be utilized to the fullest extent. When people are encouraged to assist in identifying goals and objectives in the planning stage, it is more likely that they will understand, communicate, and support the end result. Commitment to the plan flows from a sense of ownership. Clearly stated objectives and common criteria for review will encourage constructive evaluation of the program and creative planning for future action.

Every event or program, regardless of the specific purpose for which it exists, provides the opportunity to strengthen the basic leadership skills of the participants. There is an ever present objective, although often not specifically stated, to build up and equip the people of God for their ministry to the world. While planning and implementing Christian education activities, there is opportunity to identify the skills that are needed for ministry and to provide the practice of those skills in a variety of settings. Some skill areas are, for example, problem solving, group process, program planning, and conflict management.

These guidelines are offered to Christian educators but can be used by all who work in the church. The basic test question for all church leaders is, "Are my plans and the way in which I carry them out consistent with my theological principles?" The validity of the guidelines offered here will be established only if they are useful in clarifying and strengthening the activities of parish life. Perhaps they will also be an invitation to others to write their own.

4

Daring to Learn

by RICHARD A. BOWER

Frederick Buechner once wrote with some obvious simplicity that "theology is the study of God and his ways." He went on to muse: "For all we know, dung beetles may study man and his ways and call it humanology. If so, we would probably be more touched and amused than irritated. One hopes that God feels likewise." (*Wishful Thinking*, Harper & Row, 1973.)

There is always something amusing, if necessary, about humankind trying to "learn" about God, who in essential ways is beyond our "knowing." Even discussion about a "theology" of Christian education is a backhanded admission of our deep limitations, because God, not education, should be the object of our reasoning (logos). It is usually much easier to talk about how we come to know God, than to talk about God himself, the goal of our "knowing."

Reflection on learning, however, is a way, though at best a penultimate way, of reflecting upon God. For the God who *Is* (in the Biblical tradition), is a God who chooses to disclose himself, he chooses to be more than amused at our God-reasonings (theo-logos). He somehow has a vested interest in this special learning process, as One who wants to be "known," to be the Light in our darkness, the Disclosure (epiphany) in the midst of our confusions, the Wisdom in our foolishness, the Truth in the midst of our falsehoods.

To ask either the question, "How do I come to know God?," or, even deeper, "What does it mean to 'know'?," is really to ask questions about God himself. Who is this Ultimate Reality that may or may not want to be known? Who am I that I should or could know God? What connection is there, if any, between God (the One known) and me (the knower)? And does God know (or want to know) me, as well?

Like the dung beetle daring to know humankind, I dare to want to learn, to hope to learn about the one Reality which inescapably haunts me, keeps me always asking the question: Who is God, and how do I know him?

In Christian believing we have always had to do with *events,* with *tradition,* and with *common prayer.*

· In our attempts "to know" and "to find meaning" we have remembered and experienced events, the crucial event being the Incarnation, Jesus, his life, death, resurrection, and ascension. So our learning has had to do with history, especially with the history of Jesus the Christ.

· In our attempt "to know" and "to find meaning" we have had to do with tradition, the varied fabric of ways of reflecting upon and bearing witness to the sacred events, of touching their reality, of passing on their meaning and memory, of keeping us open to their present reality. Our learning has had to do with Holy Scripture, with custom and structures, with symbols connecting us with the past, giving us focus in the present and hints about our future.

In our attempt "to know" and "to find meaning" we have had to do with common prayer, with the *lex orandi* which unfolds to us the *lex credendi*. Prayer and belief (knowing) hold hands: belief leading us in prayer to commitment (faith), and prayer keeping our faith open and humble, ready and willing to live before the open-endedness of "knowing" God, continuing the conversation (*dialogue*) without falling back into a mere listening to our own echo, the grasping after false and rigid securities.

History, tradition, liturgy: these are the ways we come to faith. These are the connections between the knower and the One known. For the "knowing" we speak of is the "personal knowledge" of the God who in Christ seeks to give himself to his creation, and within that creation to be friend and brother to persons, to be known as "Thou" to me.

The image of this kind of "knowing" is the "knowing" which is "learned" in the *journey*, the *story*, and the *meal*. Knowing Christ is exemplified in the Emmaus story (Luke 24:13–35). Here the disciples "learned" Christ as they journeyed, as they listened again to the story retold, and as they broke bread with their stranger-companion. Such learning invited them to personal encounter with Jesus, whom they "knew" in the burning of their hearts.

The task, then, of Christian education in the broadest possible sense, is to enable us to know Christ, and in knowing (in the personalist-Biblical sense) to become like him.

· Everything that keeps us journeying, on the road, searching,

· Everything that keeps us telling and hearing the story in, with, and under our stories,

· Everything that keeps us returning to the Meal, is a part of the educational process, and must be seen as such.

But as with many similar things, what claims the whole often belongs to nothing. To claim so much for Christian education is often to dilute the conscious, focused, intentional efforts of the Christian education enterprise. In practice, if it is everything, it is liable to be nothing.

The ancient Greeks, from whom much of the vocabulary and philosophy of Christian education has come, had at best a sense of the wholeness of the educational enterprise. They called it *paideia*. *Paideia* was the total shaping of the Greek character. *Paideia,* as education, was not a practice which concerned the individual alone: it was essentially a function of the community. And as an educational enterprise, it was concerned not simply with intellect, but with values, aesthetics, justice, faith, responsibility, courage, politics, health, freedom, and authority. As the Christian "learns Christ," so the ancient Greek sought to "learn" the ideal image of human life. Education, for the Greek, was the search for the "divine center," and was "contrasted with the centrifugal tendencies of the sophistic era, which had declared that man was the measure of all things." (Werner Jaeger, *Paideia*, Vol. III, Oxford University Press, 1944.)

But the Greeks (especially Plato) saw the need for a more limited and technical discipline, a pedagogy in the service of *paideia*. The *paidagogos* was literally the guardian of the childhood days, the constant companion, the personal manager, the trainer in ideals and morals, the one who accompanied the child to his teachers, the "sheep dog" constantly nipping at the heels, the practical pointer to people, things, and events where learning could take place. The highest goal of the pedagogue was to make his charge eventually independent of his care—the child, as adult, to be the manager of his own learning.

St. Paul in Galatians 3:24–25, says that the Torah was our *paidagogos* to lead us to Christ. After faith we no longer are under a *paidogogos*. This is true on one level. In Christ we have come of age.

On another level, however, we still need a "school master," a way to learn Christ. This, I think, is the function of Christian education in the more specific sense. The Christian education enterprise, on whatever age level, is the intentional manager of our learning. It is the process whereby we are kept aware of the "places" we can learn. It is the process by which we learn to be learners of Christ. It is the process by which we are prodded to keep on learning. It is the way we name and are enabled to strengthen the many kinds of Christian learning that take place: in study, in choosing, in being together, in acting, in withdrawing, in thinking, in praying, in recalling. It is the process that serves as a goad, to stir up the easy complacencies of faith, to enable doubting to do its work of keeping faith awake and moving, as Frederick Buechner has written. It is often the art of learning to ask the deepest questions.

If, in the words of Thomas Groome, in his article "Shared Praxis," the goal of our Christian education is to "enable people to become decision-makers who exercise their freedom as God's children in creating with him and each other their future," then the pedagogue tries to keep a low profile, to become as unnecessary as possible. "Freedom in Christ" means not the cessation of learning and growing, but the choosing of responsibility for, not dependency in, this on-going learning.

It is a long way from the dung bettle's study of human-kind to our sense of learning to know God (theology). The difference is that God in Christ has created (or restored) a bond between Creator and creature. The blinding mystery of this "image of God" in which we share through the Spirit is the place where by faith we trust that "knowing," as well as "being known" will happen. The joyful, if awesome, attention paid to this "knowing" is the task of Christian education.

5

A Theology of Life

by FRIEDA CARNELL

It is not possible for me to formulate a theology of Christian education separate from my basic philosophy or theology of life. Therefore, that is where I must begin this essay.

I learned somewhere in my studies that theology is "faith seeking understanding." That is, through reflecting on my life and my world through the perspective of faith, an ever-growing concept of God and his being, I continue to discover new life and new perspectives. For me, this is the root of theology. My consciousness was informed many years ago by Douglas Rhymes' *Prayer in the Secular City.* I heard him saying that prayer is not just the words we use in our conscious times of talking with God, but the fullness of our lives as we live in the constant presence of God. My prayer may be joyful or sad, selfish or caring, angry or good humored, or any other mean or extreme of human emotion. But whatever I am experiencing in this life is my prayer—the living out of my relationship with God. All of this, my life, my experiences, my deepening understandings, my stretching knowledge, is a part of the information on which my theology, my continuing quest for a life more in union with my creator and the creation, is stimulated.

The theological search is supported by the awareness

that my life is lived out in the presence of God. Even when I am separated from that awareness, God is not separated from me. I often feel God pulling me to become more than I am; pulling me continuously toward a fuller, freer, more open life-style, more sensitive and responsive to creation and the pains and joys of his children. I believe that if we will open ourselves to his urgings, God will stretch our lives, our perspectives, our awarenesses. He will call us to continuously change, grow, and challenge.

We are given the example and the Word, the way and the means, in the life of Jesus. Jesus shows us a life that is not fearful of confronting the establishment, is not afraid to speak out and act against unjust treatment of persons and corruption in power. He exhibits a life that takes time to care for people as individuals. He spent much time in fellowship with his disciples—his friends; he took time to stop and teach and be with individuals in their pain—the sick, the distraught, the bereaved; he stopped to gather the children around him to tell them stories. And he enjoyed the relaxation of a good party, sometimes incurring the wrath of some who accused him of wasting time and drinking too much with persons who were "not good enough for him."

I experience a God who has ordained that this life be lived at its fullest: in awareness of our relationship with him, in awareness of his presence in each person we meet, in awareness of his presence in us. A life in which we are to laugh with his children as they play, to weep with his people in their pain and sorrow. We are to keep our eyes, ears, and hearts open to his presence in our midst as he is present in each of us and in each person we meet. We are to share the pains and joys of our brothers and sisters as he shares our pains on the cross.

We are reminded that what we do for any one of God's children, we have done for God himself.

The Word and the example for this style of life are very present in the lives of those who have heard and responded to God through the ages: the prophets of the Old Testament, Jesus and his followers in the New Testament, and the many men and women who have lived in his presence through the last twenty centuries.

We listen to Jesus tell us that he has come that we might have life more abundantly. He is with us to free us from our captivity, whether that captivity is physical or psychological. He has freed us from sin and from enslavement to the law. He has provided a new hope, a new perspective: grace and redemption.

How can we come to know and to live in that relationship with him? It surely is one of our major dichotomies that though we have been freed through Christ's resurrection, we continue to live as though we are tied to this world's demands and limitations. We ask God for forgiveness of our sins and continue to carry the burden of them in our lives. It so often seems that we hear the words with our ears, but are not able to incorporate them in our lives and hearts. *Lord, we believe, help our unbelief!*

In order to be consistant with this theology, Christian education must become a living, experienced reality within the Christian community. Christian education is a continuing, lifelong process. It is necessary for the church and its individual members to overcome their timidity in witnessing to the Good News of Jesus and God's continuing redemption of this world and our lives. Those of us who are called by the name Christian need to declare and define what that name means to us as we live out our experiences in this life and help one another reflect on our relationship with God and his son in the light of the scriptures, tradition, and contemporary insight.

Christian education is not just the burden of a few dedicated teachers and the children who are placed in their care, but the obligation of every baptized Christian. There needs to be time and opportunity for us to identify and learn from our various experiences of God in our lives. We need to share and listen to one another and hear God's many differing ways of speaking and acting through us in this world. The experiential education model is a helpful framework in which to approach this task. Very few of us have taken the time or opportunity to reflect on our lives theologically. Few have a community with which we can analyze life's experiences in the light of the Gospel, tradition, and contemporary insight, and identify how God might be trying to act in our individual and corporate lives. God invites us to be his Body in this world, to be his hands and his voice, to be his heart and his strength. But we often miss the invitation and the opportunity because we are not attuned to hear his invitation. Through identifying with others the opportunities that we had, whether acted upon or missed, and going through the process of identifying and analyzing what happened and why we were able to respond or what might have blocked response, and then sharing how awareness might be sharpened and actions be more appropriate, we will be enabled to more fully respond to God's call to serve him in this world.

Jesus chose twelve disciples to be his close companions, to learn from him and after his crucifixion and resurrection to continue to grow and develop in their ministries and understanding as they worked together and confronted one another in their differences. Study-discussion-reflection groups need to have these differences incorporated in their membership. The question of a child can broaden our range of thinking. There are also times when homogeneity is helpful in our search and identification. Continuing Christian education needs to provide the flexibility for both. Sometimes groups would be made up of persons with similar experience and expectation—at other times there would be an intentional mixture of perspectives. Like the pieces of a kaleidoscope, shifting and providing new beauty at each turn, individuals discover new facets of themselves as they interact with different groups. It is important that every member of such groups both hear and be heard across differences. The skills of active listening and asking questions for clarification would need to be developed. We would learn to be tellers of the story—the Christ story, the God story—as it has been handed to us through our heritage and as it is being acted out in our daily living.

As we learn to share the Christ story with one another in the community of his Body, we will be enabled to more effectively witness to him in the world. As we discover others who share our concerns and our joys, we will develop the kind of supportive community from which it is possible to move into the pain of God's people in our cities and towns, the nation and the world, and risk allowing him to act through us as he struggles to continually redeem the world he created.

Over the last four years, my theological perspective has been enriched by writings in the area of liberation theology. I find these insights both spiritually and socially freeing, as well as providing a fresh and freeing look at scripture. Both Old and New Testaments deal with the liberation of persons from both spiritual and physical bondage. Jesus liberates us from the burden of fear and sin, frees us to risk, explore, stretch, discover, and grow, knowing that the errors made in the process are forgiven and redeemed through the unexplainable, everpresent love of God. Then liberation from fear of rejection and reprisal can follow, as we seek to free God's oppressed and powerless children from a society that would deny them the fullness of life: liberation to combat the political and social forces that continue to oppress the poor, the uneducated, the aged, teens, women, non-"white-skinned" persons, and others in our communities and in the world.

This is what I hear in the Gospel message: The Good News we are called to live and to share with the community of faith and the world.

> *Broken*
> *Body of Christ*
> *My brother—my sister in pain*
> *Christ in pain.*

> *Healing*
> *Holding one another*
> *Christ in me joining Christ in you*
> *One in his body, united in his spirit.*

> *Growing*
> *Sharing and learning together*
> *Discovering new dimensions*
> *Of God and his redemption.*

> *Celebrate*
> *Fellowship in the Body of Christ*
> *Diverse in experience and perspective*
> *One in spirit.*

6

Education for Christian Living

by DOUGLAS T. COOKE

I think of Christian education as education for Christian living. It is a dynamic process involving all of life and includes, as essential, the dimension of action engaging each of us in a relationship with God and with each other.

Thus understanding grows out of the conviction that God is at work in his world, touching people's lives through the power of the Spirit. As people move day by day through the world God has created, they continually encounter his presence, often in surprising places; and they witness to others of their own experience of his love and forgiveness. Just as individuals' daily lives are ongoing, so too is their encounter with *The Life*. The knowledge and experience of the presence of God is never completed.

Education for Christian living grows out of an incarnational understanding of God. As God made himself known in the supreme incarnational event—in the person of Jesus Christ in a particular place, at a particular time, in the day-to-day lives of a particular people, so, too, does he make himself known now in the lives of people in ways they can see and hear and touch and feel.

In this view of Christian education, all of life is part of the educational process. Every occasion, every encounter, every experience is the locus of learning. A child's polio shot and a healing miracle both partake of the mercy of God. The birth of a child and the story of Genesis are aspects of the creative activity of God. There is no separation between what is "religious" or "Christian" and what is not.

The task is to hold all of this up and to look at it from a perspective and an overview which says that this is God's world and he is at work in it. It requires an enabling function and is aimed at opening minds and hearts and vision to see that God is where people are.

If Christian education of this kind is to take place, there must be thoughtful and careful preparation. Today most Christian educators understand that for education to be effective, it must grow out of the local situation and be developed to meet the unique opportunities and needs existing in a specific congregation. This is often misunderstood. It is thought to be an excuse for avoiding serious content or for evading the responsibility of dealing with the existence of eternal truth. This could not be further from the truth. Good Christian education cannot have an amorphous content. If one takes seriously the call to develop such programs of Christian education within a parish, it requires that a total view be taken—a view which includes:

1. The Biblical content
2. The historical experiences the church has had of the activity of God
3. The faith experiences of the individuals involved
4. The personal and world life-issues

These components are included in all good written curricula, but too often curriculum is chosen without any reference to the life and activity of the congregation and its people. When this is done, the essential dimension is missing.

But it is important to note that when the responsibility of the educational program is given to each local situation, a serious question needs to be raised. How can the local congregation be sure that it has a content which fully expresses the faith? Sometimes, in its enthusiasm, a congregation with good resources of money and people will design a unique educational program which may have a blind spot or an exaggeration of the truth. Or a congregation with a lack of resources might have a limited program which could gain by stretching and new vision. Such concerns have much historical precedent. One just needs to read St. Paul's letters to the local congregations of the early church to find examples of these age-old problems.

I believe that whenever such a responsibility is given to a part of the church, there needs to be a method to provide a corrective. Although this word often has a negative connotation, I see including the sense of enlarging, stretching, and opening, as well as that of setting perameters.

One way the early church found its corrective was through St. Paul's guidance in the form of letters. Today I see this question being addressed through interdependent activity. I see the method to deal with this is to insure that the individual units interact with each other. This kind of interdependent activity is essential and must be encouraged if there is to be a wholeness to the religious education programs of the churches.

Often there is resistance to this on the part of the "successful" congregations because they see this as another demand upon their time and resources. The congregations with less defined programs of education often come away from such gatherings with a sense of failure or of having learned about something which won't work for them.

The heart of the problem is the *agenda* of such meetings or interactions. Methodology, resources, models, procedures, curricula may be useful appendices, but the main task is to share answers to questions such as these:

· What is it we teach and why?
· Why have we made our choice of what we teach?
· What do we wish to have happen in the lives of those who are involved in this teaching and learning experience?

These questions are of equal importance to everyone. And we can learn from each other. This interaction can be the corrective which is absolutely necessary to our overall philosophy of Christian education.

Another responsibility Christian educators have is to provide people with a way to relate the information about and content of Christianity to their lives. If we are talking about education for Christian living, information *about* the Christian faith is of little significance without a context or a way to make it relevant. Multitudes of people know *facts* about the Christian faith, some of them quite correct, but many of them partial truths, or incorrect. The problem is that for many people this body of "facts" or of information is so fragmentary and so unrelated to the larger core that there is little to hold onto or "come back" to. Christian education's failure to relate to life, or to have a methodology to make it relate, or to supply the understanding and experience in a Christian community to assist and support, will make the most important factual information ultimately empty words, with no power for salvation.

The greatest opportunity Christian educators have today is to help break down the walls which have enclosed the educational ministry. It has usually been assumed by virtually everyone that Christian education is for the nurture of children. Today we have a new experience. Adults throughout the church are beginning to look for opportunities to learn. God the Holy Spirit is stirring the minds and hearts of his people to learn and to witness.

One important aspect of this is to take seriously the role of the Christian community as a body of people who can support each other in their faith development. The ethos and the norms of our church life have, in most places, precluded any kind of gathering to share what people believe and what the faith means in their lives. Such opportunities need to be developed on a regular and serious basis. These gatherings will reinforce what people know, expand their vision, and correct misunderstandings. Then in the day-to-day world, when they are confronted with questions or called upon to witness, they have, as well as the presence of the living God, a group of people who have shared and worked with them to discover the truth of the love and forgiveness of God.

7

Christian Education
as Revelation

by SYLVAN HEATH

My children have outgrown the love of riddles, but I haven't. Here is a family favorite:

Q: Where does King Kong sleep?
A: Any place he wants to.

And a variation:

Q: How does God reveal himself?
A: Any way he wants to.

Christian education, like all education, has to do with knowledge. But this knowledge is of a unique kind: the knowledge of God. It depends entirely upon God's revelation of himself to his people. "Revelation is not a theological concept similar to others," says Gabriel Moran, "but instead a premise for theological construction as a whole."

As church educators we assume that the church is in a special way a vessel of God's self-disclosure. Through the church, he reveals his nature and his expectations of us. He manifests himself to the world through his church—and to the church through his world. Our responsibility as educators is to cooperate with him to the end that his people may be reconciled with him and with each other. In this paper I want to look at Christian education in terms of revelation, using the structure of Avery Dulles's models of the church. God reveals himself any way he wants to, and the five models are a useful, if limited, means of looking at some of the ways in which Christian educators can cooperate with God's action.

The Church as Institution. In the institutional model of the church, revelation is seen as once-for-all. The church conserves and transmits apostolic teaching. It does so by the authority conferred on it by its Lord, who himself "taught as one who had authority." The institutional church, moreover, gives structure and continuity to the "content" of the other models. In its doctrines it formalizes the beliefs of the church, and in its history it embodies the stories of the people of God.

Perhaps the greatest challenge to church educators today is to find ways of communicating these beliefs and stories. One is astounded over and over again by the degree of ignorance of the church's most basic teachings. The laity are handicapped in every area of their ministry by this ignorance. Many of these intelligent, committed, ignorant people have heard hundreds of excellent sermons, which only indicates that preaching is not automatically an effective teaching method. Catechesis, especially of adults, is an obvious and primary responsibility of the church educator.

The Church as Mystical Community. Dulles describes revelation, in this model, as "an aspect of the union between the human spirit and the divine. . . . Revelatory grace opens men up to one another. As men come to recognize one another as fellow recipients of the same grace, they gather to form the Church." Revelation comes through relationships and process.

Educators can play two roles within this model. Their skills in group process and communication can be placed at the service of community-building and of sustaining healthy life in the community. And, in addition to these skills, their understanding of effective educational methods can aid in the communication of the beliefs which bind the members together.

The Church as Sacrament. Many Episcopalians find great power in this model of the church. The church as sacrament links the first two models; it is mystical communion made visible in institutional form. It reflects and bridges two ways in which God reveals himself: in interior, spiritual encounter, and in visible symbolization, "words or deeds, creed or sacrament" (Dulles).

The "faith enculturation" model of John Westerhoff is one example of Christian education at work within the church-as-sacrament model. "Our faith experiences are always translated (and need to be) into religious beliefs," says Westerhoff in *Learning Through Liturgy.* "This process of institutionalization involves the symbolic transformation of the experience of God. . . ." The community of faith is the context for Christian education, and the means are "the actions between and among faithful persons" (*Will Our Children Have Faith?*). Participation in liturgy is an essential way in which education takes place. This is not to say that liturgy is merely a teaching device, nor is participation in liturgy automatically an educational experience. Rather, through intentional planning, educational experiences can help people see and use what is happening in liturgy.

The Church as Herald. In the kerygmatic model, Jesus Christ, the Word of God, is the source of revelation, and the church is mediator. The church is called to proclaim the Good News revealed in Christ and in salvation history, as recorded in the Bible.

This includes the evangelistic and the preaching modes of the church's life. The task of the educator is *not* to be an evangelist, but to equip the evangelists. Those who are called to proclaim the Gospel need first to know the story of Jesus: who he was, what he did, what he claimed to be, why his living power is among us now. Second, they need skills and practice in communicating this story, in linking it to their own stories, and in listening and responding to those to whom they are witnessing. Preaching from the pulpit is likewise an aspect of the church's kerygmatic activity; it might be noted that many clergy could be better equipped to communicate the gospel as teachers and preachers.

The Church as Servant. Revelation, in the diaconal model, is not once-for-all, but is on-going. The church is to be open to God's self-disclosure through the people and events around us, "to interpret the many voices of our age, judging them in the light of the divine Word" (Dulles). Conversely, God is revealed to the world through the evidence of the coming of his kingdom, a kingdom of justice and liberation.

Education for liberation, one aspect of this model, includes "consciencization," the process whereby individuals and groups, by relating their own circumstances to the Gospel, are empowered to move toward freedom. It suggests educational methods such as Wink's "Bible study for human transformation," and Groome's "praxis," with its reflection-encounter-decision dynamic. The servant model also calls for education which sensitizes Christians to the needs of the world, informs them of the realities, and enables them to serve effectively and intelligently (rather than with the romantic idealism which is a risk of Christian social action).

Relationship of the Five Models to Each Other—and to Christian Education. Dulles does not "absolutize" any one model. Thomas Downs, in *The Parish as Learning Community,* says that an ideal parish has elements of all models, and that they may serve as corrective to one another: "In the least evident models are the promise of greatest potential." Dulles sees their integration as taking place within the paradigm of one of the models: ". . . one may then work backward and integrate into this model the values of the other four."

It is particularly appropriate that educators should be aware of the strengths and weaknesses of each model, and of their potential for reinforcing or balancing each other. For example, evangelists need to have an understanding of the place of the institutional church, both as the context for Biblical revelation and as the structure within which converts will live out their discipleship. Similarly, sound teaching of the doctrine of man and of sin may be needed to balance an emphasis on the servant church. On the other hand, the educator's sensitivity to people's needs for community and for personal experience of God's reality may be brought to bear on an excessively institutional, "content-centered" program. The convictions and methods of liberation-oriented theology can serve as a balance to a sacramentally- or community-oriented parish which might be tempted to float off into otherworldliness. In ways such as these, the Christian educator who is theologically aware (and also sensitive and diplomatic!) may even have an influence on church life which goes far beyond the obviously "educational."

I have described Christian educators rather objectively, primarily as technicians whose skills are placed in God's service to enable his people to grow in their faith and to do the work of the church. But if we do these things *only* as technicians, we will severely limit our potential for serving as a channel of God's revelation.

What I have to offer others is first of all who I am—not what I can do. I am drawn to the sacramental and communal descriptions of the church because it is here that the Living Christ moves most tangibly in the midst of his people. It is here that I find God's revelation of himself as Person, not as a body of facts or moral imperatives. In this relationship with Christ I become the person he means me to be; I am enabled not merely to teach Christianity to others, but to be Christian with others and, with grace, for others.

8

Toward Relationship With God

by ELIZABETH B. HIGH

"Man was not created in jest or at random."

There is a standard Middle Eastern dish which is wholly nutritious and a delicious meal in itself. It is also served to introduce a larger meal or a banquet and is always offered as a symbol of hospitality. My son-in-law, who provided the opportunity for me to discover the dish, tells me it is as common in the Middle East as cornflakes or peanut butter are in the United States.

The dish is served as a matter of course. Thousands of years of experience, culture, and intuition preclude the necessity of explaining to anyone that it is basic, that it serves nutritional requirements, satisfies appetite, assuages the hunger of the moment and is life-sustaining. From time to time when agricultural or seasonal abberration dictate, some of the ingredients are left out. This is disaster. Without all of the ingredients, it just "doesn't work." The subtle interplay of one component with the others is necessary to produce the whole. It is the combination upon which people depend for nurture and from which they derive satisfaction.

Feta cheese and bread are the mainstays of the dish. A thick slice of tomato is placed on the cheese, topped with a slice of onion. Cured black olives are heaped on the side with the bread. If there are no olives, or tomatoes are not in season, the onion dominates and the cheese becomes barely digestible. If the onion is omitted, the olives are too acid and the rest of the combination becomes bland. Without the cheese or the bread, there is no balance in the nutrition and long-term deprivation may lead to illness and death. Constant searching about for bits of this or that to substitute in the combination destroys the essence, complicates the balance, and produces an undifferentiated mishmash.

Thousands of years of experience, culture, and intuition preclude the necessity of explaining to anyone that becoming "educated" in one's religion is basic, that it serves nurturing requirements, satisfies appetite, assuages the hunger of the moment, and is life-sustaining. The longing for that which we are not, the seeking for that which we would become is innate, inescapable—a comes-with-the-package fact of being human. The revelation, the opportunity for discovery that the longing and seeking, the need, is for relationship with God—this is the task of religious education. The process of religious education leads one to discover an unending variety of ways to come into relationship with God.

From time to time when societal catastrophe or aberration of trends dictate, some of the ingredients of Christian education are left out. This is disaster. Without all of the ingredients, it just "doesn't work." The subtle interplay of one component with the others is necessary to produce the whole. It is the combination upon which people depend for nurture and from which they derive satisfaction.

Faith and worship are the mainstays. Prayer, relationship, and opportunity for discovery are combined within the context of the worshipping community. Together they are nurturing by themselves or can introduce a larger dimension or "banquet" of religious experience. If there are no opportunities provided for discovery or the relationships are based on falsity or unsound values, the worship becomes barely comprehensible. If prayer is omitted the discovery opportunities become bland; without faith and worship there is no balance in the nurturing and long-term deprivation can lead to illness and death. Constant searching about for bits of this or that to substitute in the combination destroys the essence, complicates the balance, and produces an undifferentiated mishmash.

Just as feta cheese is developed out of an environment in which natural processes are allowed to take place to produce an effect upon a natural substance, so faith develops. When humans seek to construct a new thing they create an elaborate set of blueprints. When God seeks to construct a new thing he starts with a seed. So says H. C. N. Williams, the provost of Coventry. Thomas Merton writes in *New Seeds of Contemplation,* "For just as the wind carries thousands of winged seeds, so each moment brings with it germs of spiritual vitality that come to rest imperceptibly in the minds and wills of men." The innate necessity for relationship with an *essential other* provides the ground for the seeds of faith. Religious education seeks to interpret the moments of life in which the germs of spiritual vitality, the seeds of faith, may develop and grow, strengthen and flourish to satisfy man's devastating emptiness without relationship with God. "God is the 'Thou' before whom our inmost 'I' springs into awareness . . . faith puts the intellect into possession of Truth which reason cannot grasp by itself." (Merton, ibid.)

From the earliest traces of mankind on earth, we discover that man is a worshipping being. The constant need to relate to that which is beyond, above, other-than is the raw material of Christian education. Just as our Lord constantly invites us to take, to eat the bread of his body, so must we be "in" worship to do so. Earliest man needed to make something up to worship. Christian education is the process by which the accumulated experience of God's revelation of himself to man supercedes the need to "make something up." The unutterable privilege of response to God's revelation of himself in Jesus Christ in the context of the Eucharist is simply consistent with what God created man to do—what man has been seeking to do since the dawn of time: worship the author of the universe.

Prayer may be the newest frontier of religious development. In terms of reason, intellect, and shared experience perhaps more is known about prayer than any other facet of religion. In terms of the "Thou" before whom our inmost "I" springs into awareness, prayer is the leading edge of discovery. If the process of religious education is to include opportunities for discovery, prayer is the entry, the road map, and sometimes the grab-bag of surprises. And prayer is a little like tomatoes. Prayer can be neatly sectioned off, sometimes contains bitter seeds, is cool green when immature and rich and savory when allowed to ripen. Whatever it is that God would have man become is very closely touched in prayer. As the disciplines of science and theology begin to merge and man's spiritual nature is being studied by sophisticated photography and electronic equipment, we can only become more and more aware of the complexity and variety of this vital link to wholeness.

Man was not created in jest or at random. God has provided those elements and combinations of elements which nurture and sustain. The onion spice of relationships, the risk and acid of olives and discovery alike are components of a whole. Religious education is the endeavor by which, in relationship with the worshipping community, God's revelation of himself to man is interpreted, apprehended, and is the propelling force by which his lambs are fed.

9

Education of the Easter People

by JACK HILYARD

So the Word became flesh; he came to dwell among us and we saw his glory, such glory as befits the Father's only Son, full of grace and truth.

(John 1:14)

Consecrate them by the truth; thy word is truth.

(John 17:17)

As the Father sent me, so I send you.

(John 20:21)

We are Easter people—a part of the resurrection community. We are given life and love: Life with the fullest potential possible; love to support whoever we are and whatever we might do. We are renewed, renewing, and renewers. Through our baptism into the resurrection of Jesus Christ we are renewed. Our lives are open to change. We are open to new possibilities. Each of us is given special gifts, talents, and abilities. We are given power to continue to be a part of God's on-going, renewing creation. We are sent into the world to renew those parts of the world that our lives touch.

In the 17th chapter of St. John's gospel, Jesus prays for his followers. This is a powerful prayer in that Jesus describes his ministry and asks God's protection, care, and guidance that the ministry continue through those who follow. He prays:

—that we may know God;
—that we know Jesus is of God;
—that we may know love;
—that we may be one;
—that we may be consecrated in his word—truth;
—and that we may be sent into the world.

These affirmations I would make:

—We are loved by God.
—We know this love through the sacraments and through the community of faith.
—We are given a community for support and nurture.
—God is active in the world—transforming and renewing his creation.
—We are sent into the world and we meet God there.
—We have been given the Spirit for guidance.
—We each have special gifts, talents, skills, and abilities to offer. As we offer them they are blessed.

These affirmations are not unique to Christian education, but are understandings for the whole church. It seems appropriate to give some thought to the church—the community of faith. Two quotations from Scripture seem significant:

St. Peter, preparing to preach to the very young church quotes the prophet Joel. His words are important to us today:

Your sons and daughters will proclaim my message: Your young men will see visions and your old men will have dreams. Yes, even on my servants, both men and women, I

*will pour out my Spirit in those days, and they will proclaim
my message.*

(Acts 2:17b–18)

The second is a realization of those people in the early
church as they began to take God's message into the
world. They had many gifts to offer:

*And these were his gifts: some to be apostles, some prophets,
some evangelists, some pastors and teachers, to equip God's
people for work in his service, to the building up of Christ's
body.*

(*Ephesians 4:11–12*)

In considering life within this community of faith and a
ministry and mission to the world we make certain assumptions about the community:

THAT THERE BE A COMMUNITY:
—in which one meets the Lord, in which the Spirit
  dwells, and through which creation and redemption
  continues;
—which gathers for worship and support, and which
  scatters for its work in the world;
—which is expressive of the unity of God.

THAT WE LEARN TO LOVE AND TRUST:
—that we have faith in God's message.
—that we know God's love and the love of our fellow
  Christians.

THAT THERE BE STORYTELLERS, DREAMERS, AND VISION-
ARIES:
—that we may hear, experience, and rejoice in the stories of faith from our heritage and that we might
  share our own journeys in faith;
—that we might be led on mission through a vision of
  a changed and renewed world;

—that we might claim our gifts for mission and ministry.

These assumptions are not unique to Christian education; they are a part of the whole church as it sets out to "equip God's people" for life within the community and for mission and ministry in the world.

As a discipline Christian education (religious education/church education) is at a crossroads. We need a new set of definitions, assumptions, and affirmations. The old words have been captured and imprisoned in a set of assumptions that tell us Christian education is the schooling of children. Our model for Christian education has been the secular school and our approach has been the transferring of a body of information from one person to another. The teacher has determined what the student needs to learn. This model is no longer appropriate as it carries with it assumptions and implications that hinder the task.

If our task is "equipping God's people" for mission and ministry within the community and in the world (and I believe it is), we need to look as a whole church for new models. We might begin by asking some foundational questions. How do we prepare ourselves and others to minister within the community? How do we prepare for mission in the world? Have we ever asked adults or children what they need or want to learn? Have we asked what skills are needed to be a people on mission?

In building a new model we need to ask ourselves: How can we be Christian together? How do we share this faith with a broken world? How is God's revelation known in the particular task? In asking these questions we will be searching for new models; the old ones will not be helpful. In the process of creating or discovering new models, we may do things in radically different ways. But we also may help people discover and claim their ministry. We may redefine the roles within the household of faith.

I am convinced that there will be a stronger community of faith as the stories and understandings are shared. We will be more intentional about our ministry in the community and our mission in the world. We'll be working as the whole church offering those gifts to the upbuilding of Christ's Body.

In writing this paper I have discovered:

—that there is not a separate theology for Christian education; rather there is a theology for the church with implications for Christian education.

—that it is vital that our understandings of the task of the church be firmly based in Scripture.

—that in recent history we have cut the church into several pieces. The time has come to see how those separate pieces fit together and work together.

—that our model for Christian education need not be the secular school, yet we would do well to understand and to make use of educational theory, techniques and skills from secular education.

—that a theological statement is something "in process." It grows out of one's faith experience and as such will change from time to time and with the experience within the community of faith.

10

Religious Education—
A Mosaic

by FRED J. HOWARD

"What did I do to deserve this?" "Why is this happening to me?" "I think God may be trying to tell me something." "Why me, Lord, why me?" "What will be, will be."

Questions and statements like the ones above are the beginnings of theological processes. Such questions and statements are also part of the religious education endeavor.

To ponder the power, intent, and integrity of a being greater than one's self is to think theologically. The thinking may be based on speculation, superstition, dogma, doctrine, creed, beliefs, knowledge, or any combination of these and others, but to think about god, any god (of any name) is to think theologically.

To seek answers to such pondering is religious education. The act or process of imparting or gaining knowledge about that which is religious is "religious education." And I agree with Joseph Russell who says, "the task of religious education is to raise questions—not provide answers."

The theology of religious education is, then, the quest or journey of God's people living out the mysteries of life and creation in intentional ways of searching. We never know all there is to know, especially when we think we do. Purposeful and intentional ways of finding new knowledge should be a part of religious education. The lack of intent is similar to looking for something with our eyes closed.

Sometimes we stumble into things and discover them accidently, but discovery comes more easily when we open our eyes and search systematically (even if we are not sure of that for which we are searching). Likewise, religious education takes place even when no one is concerned about that the individual may be learning—or how—but its quality (and accuracy) is up to chance.

Christian education is a part of religious education. Just as the Christ Event did not occur by itself, unrelated to history, nor in a closed system, neither does a Christian's education concern only the Christian aspects of history, present or future. This may become a major focus for Christian educators in the next decade.

If the world's major religions all have common goals about peace, the welfare of mankind, and the stewardship of the earth (and there is good evidence to presume this is true), one major task of Christian education will be to provide a religious education enabling Christians to help in the goal attainment. This will not involve the question of "who's going to heaven?" (though that might be an interesting theological question), but "how can we better our participation in God's ongoing creation?"

Most religious education—certainly Christian education—is unique. Unique, that is, in comparison to other education systems. Let me use Christian education as an example to explain what I mean by "unique."

Education in technology, science, or the arts is concerned primarily with facts, equations, formulas, etc. That is, at any given point in time a society or culture (or sub-group) has accumulated a compilation of "hard data" which can be used by people for their betterment and the betterment of others. The purpose of education is to impart as much of this hard data as possible to the next generation so that it can both use it and improve it. The data that is learned is used over and over again until it is changed or replaced.

The goal of Christian education is relationships: with self; with God; with neighbor; with society; and with the world. Any information (data) which is passed from generation to generation is done so as to enhance the relationships and understanding of relationships. Further, each encounter with any of these interdependent relationships is unique in and of itself. Others may be similar, but time, space, experience, or spirit always make each interaction different.

For Christian education, relationship (person and God; person and person) are primary and facts are secondary. For education in its normal sense (secular education), facts are primary and relationships (though of some concern) are secondary. The distinction lies in the fact that relational education is not done in the same way as factual education.

Christian education is done by the learner—not the teacher. The Christian educator provides ways in which the learner may examine his or her own series of relationships within the Christian context. To do this, the more teachers of Christian education know about how persons learn, the better they can provide such ways. Striving for memorized or attained facts—Ten Commandments, creeds, Bible heroes, church history, or denominational doctrine—may give the learner a good set of guide lines and sign posts for her or his faith journey. But until the student has a chance to see or experience those facts in action in relationships with the self, God, neighbor, society, and the world, the education is incomplete.

The goal of Christian education (or, better, religious education for Christians) is to enable Christian people to live in self esteem as God's people who are constantly being called into a community of Christ. The theology of Christian education is the theology of the church, the "community of God's people." For each generation to become the community, it must be nurtured in how that community interrelates. That nurturing is done by a combination of the Holy Spirit and religious education.

So far, our focus has been primarily on religious education and the individual's relationship with self, God, neighbor, society, and the world. This cannot be done by an individual alone. The community of God's people as a body is where religious education takes place. In a community where faith, hope, love, forgiveness, and atonement are the main dynamics of relationships, each member of the community both teaches and learns from all other members: young and old; female and male; lay and ordained; and all other contrasting categories found or forced in communities.

"Community," as a word and as a concept, is overused and misused. It has become the byword and goal of many gatherings. ("If we can only achieve 'community' before we leave, the conference will be a success!") One would think that community is a state of being similar to gelatin when it hardens or corn when it is ready to be plucked from the stalk.

Community in the Biblical sense is not a static plateau from which a group announces, "By Jove, I think we've got it!" It is rather an amoebalike entity, with diverse relationships causing tensions and supports, pulls and pushes, that finds strength in the openness of its diversity. A better analogy, used by Paul, is the body—diverse, always changing, mutually, interdependent on the many parts and their relationships.

Much has been written and said about the marks of a Christian community. I would probably agree (at least in part) with most schemata. From the perspective of religious education, I find the following to be a way of grasping the dynamics of the Christian community.

1. *The Story:* The ongoing miracle of the Christian Gospel that God through Christ allows people of each age to become a part of God's story. That story is dramatic and filled with spectacular relationships. Most of the people in the story are ordinary people who respond to relationships with God and others in love, and find extraordinary results. It is an unfinished mosaic of God weaving through history and the lives of people, waiting for each person to add his or her story to the color and pattern of the weave.

2. *Worship:* Worship, for the Christian, is where the past, the present, and the future are tied together. The common story, our story as it is unfolding, and the hopeful story as we see it—all of these are lifted up in offering and praise, in confession and celebration, as we worship. Worship is both subject and object of Christian education.

3. *Cause:* Christians do have a common cause. We sometimes act as if we didn't, and much of our rhetoric gives the impression that we are at odds with one another. But in spite of appearance, and perhaps enhanced by our differences, we have a common cause: to be the Body of Christ healing a broken world.

That cause is very complex. Christian education is a part of that cause while it is also a precursor to it. The cause is the "glue" that binds the community of God's people together. The cause is above each member and all members. And when an individual leaves one locale and moves to another, the story may change, worship may change, either aspect of the community may change, but the cause remains constant.

4. *Goal:* The goal of all Christians is (I believe) to strive for a world in which all of God's children can be a part of the beauty of creating and salvation instead of victims or executioners of ill will. As this goal conflicts with human nature, religious education is necessary for the conflict resolution to be accomplished.

5. *Life Together:* An easy reference for life together as Christians striving for community is the pastoral epistle of I John. The Jerusalem Bible is especially helpful with its outline and footnotes.

The whole quantitative and qualitative measure of grace—at least in this life—is how we live together. Story, worship, cause, and goal become only words if Christians do not laugh, cry, rejoice, hurt, celebrate, and grieve with each other. Even faith, hope, and love become tokens if we do not let down our barriers and assist each other in holding to God's spirit.

To engender sharing life is the task of the church. To know how is, in part, the task of religious education. It is especially in this task of Christian education that we realize facts and data are only instrumental at best in knowing the Christian life.

The theology of religious education: a loom upon which God weaves the stories of all humankind into a mosaic of atonement, characterized and colored by celebration, common cause, goal, and life together—always becoming, never ending.

11

Called to be the Church in the World

by WILLIAM F. KIRKPATRICK

At one moment I did answer "yes" to Someone or Something—and from then on I was certain that my existence was meaningful and that, therefore, my life in self surrender had a goal.

Dag Hammarskjold

To say "yes" is to commit one's life to the fact that nothing will ever be the same again because of that commitment, turning point, or change. To me, a theology of Christian education is always unfolding—revealing more fullness, more opportunity for wholeness, a more direct path to oneness with God and to a clearer understanding of what one's goal, purpose, and meaning in life might be. It is to say "yes" or "no" many times over, and over again, in the process of living. To be able to affirm human existence is to say "yes" to one's own participation in it and to be an affirmative human being. When the Christian says "yes," he or she is saying yes not only to their own life but to their neighbor's life, and to God. In affirming oneself and one's neighbor, God is affirmed at the same time.

> For Jesus Christ, who was preached among you, is not one who is 'yes' and 'no' . . . on the contrary, he is

God's 'yes'; for it is he who is the 'yes' to all of God's promises. . . . It is God himself who has set us apart, who has placed his mark of ownership upon us, and who has given us the Holy Spirit in our hearts as the guarantee of all that he has in store for us."
II Corinthians 1:19–22

You do not have to live very long to see that if a person is going to affirm life, he or she must deal with the fact of death. In 1951, in my late teens, I experienced what it meant to be near death. Paralyzed from the neck down through poliomyelitis and gasping for my next breath, I slipped in and out of consciousness as I was rushed from one hospital to another in an ambulance. I was aware of my mother's presence beside me during that ride. I also knew that I was critical. Unknown to me, the doctors told my parents that I might not make it through the night. My mother prayed with me and told me, "Son, we love you very much and God loves you, too. No matter what you see or hear, God will be with you always. . . . Also, remember the 23rd Psalm . . . 'the Lord is my Shepherd.' "

That same evening, I experienced the sensation of falling into a deep dark pit as I tried to get away from the pain which pounded throughout my body. I cried aloud to God to save me, for my goal was to be a doctor and to help others. I repeated the 23rd Psalm over and over, and as I repeated the Psalm, I said "yes" to God, and committed my life to whatever he had in store for me. Within myself, I knew that I was loved very much by my parents and by God, that love was enough to comfort and sustain me throughout the night, and a peacefulness came over me. I awoke the next morning, alive with God's spirit to get me through whatever I had to face.

Ten years later, while completing my clinical pastoral

education requirement at Massachusetts General Hospital in Boston, I met and spoke with the famous psychiatrist who developed logotherapy, Dr. Viktor E. Frankl, author of *From Death Camp to Existentialism, Man's Search for Meaning*. We had an opportunity to share our stories of being near death. Through his experience in Auschwitz during World War II, he concluded, "What matters is not the meaning of life in general, but rather the specific meaning of a person's life at any given moment." Dr. Frankl affirmed my beliefs about the meaning of life, and that love is the ultimate and the highest goal to which humankind can aspire. Frankl's experience led him to believe that "in accepting a challenge to suffer bravely, whether in prison or with a disease, life has a meaning up to the last moment; for life's meaning is an unconditional one for it even includes the potential meaning of suffering." He also believes that "man is basically a responsible creature and must actualize the potential meaning of his life which," says Frankl, "is to be found in the world rather than within man or his own psyche, as though it were a closed system. Human existence is essentially self-transcendence rather than self-actualization."

I share this personal story because, first of all, I believe that a theology of Christian education must enable each of us to make the connection between the story of Jesus and the writing out of our own stories. Secondly, I believe that we must share or witness to others individually and in community, the continuous working of God in the history of his people as well as in their personal histories. Thirdly, I believe that in acting out God's purpose as well as reflecting on it, we experience the creative tension which exists between nurture, or inreach, and mission, or outreach.

Let me further clarify this tension. We are called to

love God and to love our neighbors as ourselves. I believe we have to love ourselves first before we can reach out to love others. If one doesn't love oneself, i.e., the good that is within or the Christ within, then one can never love or recognize and love the Christ in others. Therefore, there is an inward journey and an outward journey one must take in order to experience and know what God's purpose might be. In order to build up the Body of Christ, we must be prepared to do Christian service.

This leads to my next point which is that the Faith Community of believers, the local congregation, must experience a creative tension between nurture and mission. A theology of Christian education should include the modeling of the four dimensions of the early church. It is never a question of *either* nurture *or* mission—but it is a question of *both* nurture *and* mission. Nurture was the partner of and training ground for *mission*. The pendulum down through the past several decades has swung from one extreme to the other. In the 50's, Christian education was on top, while the 60's were engrossed with social action to the detriment of nurturing the members of the Body. The 70's saw a resurgence of evangelism and Christian education. Let's hope the 80's express a balance and a creative tension of "both-and." A structure for a Faith Community might look like the model on page 68.

As the Faith Community experiences and models wholeness from the double expression of the four dimensions of faith, individuals within the community begin to accept more of life, become more open to themselves and to others, and learn to trust themselves and others more, thereby trusting life more. This is to trust Christ within more as the source of the life process, helping life unfold, making each person more creative,

A Structure for Congregational Life Today
that learns from the double expression of the four dimensions of faith would look like this:

NURTURE (inreach)	DIMENSIONS	MISSION (outreach)
preaching and teaching	(kerygma) TELLING	evangelism
care for the brothers and sisters	(diakonia) DOING Servanthood (Developing a caring community)	action in the world, social service & social action
life together within	(koinonia) BEING Fellowship Building	life together without
worship and sacrament	(leitourgia) CELEBRATING	festivals in the marketplace
	"DO WE HAVE IT ALL TOGETHER" "IN THE NAME OF CHRIST"	

From *Do and Tell: Engagement Evangelism in the '70s* by Gabriel Fackre.

more whole selves. To be in this process is to be in God; to trust it is to trust God; to participate in it is to participate in his story and in his action. The more we are open to ourselves and to others and to God, the more we are living in him who is life: it is to be vulnerable, to take risks, to be a fool—for Christ's sake.

I have been influenced and impressed recently by the

Center for Parish Development in Naperville, Illinois, which has developed a model of the church in ministry and mission. My theology of Christian education would include the Center's three basic assumptions about the function of the church in ministry and mission. First of all, *the church is a pilgrim people of God on a spiritual journey,* and a Christian educator's objective is to enable persons and groups to participate in a spiritual journey, intentionally proclaiming, celebrating, and deepening spiritual consciousness and meaningful relationships to God. Secondly, *the church is a caring community,* and the educator's objective is to extend the caring spirit of Jesus by developing supportive, healing, open, trusting relationships with others in which people are free to love and be loved. Thirdly, *the church is an empowering community,* and the educator's task is to enable persons and groups, in response to the call of Christ, to increase their awareness of the oppressive forces operating within and around them, to take charge of their own lives, to develop the resources and skills necessary for human liberation, and to reshape their situation.

I believe one of the tasks of Christian education is to build the Faith Community so that people can be involved in their own faith development with others. If we have any model of true community, it is in the Biblical vision of what the church *should* be. The task within that community is to help people to develop a theology which is carried out by constant reflection upon the human experience within the community of faith, as well as within the community of the secular world.

As Christians are led out of the Faith Community and back into the world, Christian education can be a process by which people are supported in their task of being change agents to overcome the oppressive forces which operate within and around them. I believe that

Christians are called to be change agents and to try to break down the barriers which block any kind of social change, namely, sexism, racism, ageism, and elitism. We are called to help people diminish their feelings of fear, guilt, anger, powerlessness, and inadequacy, so that people will be free to love one another. We are called to create an outward climate in which people are affirmed and valued, seeking justice for the oppressed, the forgotten, the isolated.

The calling out of the community to be the church in the world cannot be accomplished without people being grounded in a sense of identity which is rooted in the Biblical story. I believe this can be accomplished by reflecting intentionally on our behaviors and our actions. It's an old cliché that people learn from experience, which is at best a half-truth. Most all of us have many experiences, some over and over again, and still don't learn from them. Another school says it's the facts that count—education is accumulated information which is organized in a systematic way. But the trouble is that people don't respond appropriately, even when we have the facts. For instance, take the example of the person who continues to smoke even though he or she knows it may lead to lung cancer. Real learning takes place when experience and information are so reflected upon, so combined, as to enable a person to respond appropriately and adequately in his or her own life's situation.

A theology of Christian education can never be static, but rather is alive, ongoing, moving, exciting, and unfolding. It is found in the stories we share with one another within the Faith Community, as well as witness to our brothers and sisters in the world through caring, being vulnerable, and enabling others to attain wholeness and spiritual well-being which is developed through an interlocking chain of relationships. As the NICA definition expresses it: "Spiritual well-being is the affirmation of life in a relationship with God, self, community and environment that nurtures and celebrates wholeness."

It is such a comfort to know that St. Francis of Assisi at the very end of his life called his brothers together saying, "Come brothers, let us now begin to be Christians." What good news that is for me that you and I are always in the process of becoming Christians. That's exciting for me today to know that tomorrow will bring more growth and thus enable me to become more than I have been and strive toward what the Lord knows that I can become.

12

Change and Belief

by THOMAS J. McELLIGOTT

There are two things I want to say about this paper. First, I am writing it at the request of the Rev. David W. Perry as one assignment given to all regional religious education coordinators. The second thing I want to say is how difficult it has been for me to write this statement. I have done the paper over a number of times, and each time it changes, as I change in the process of learning what I believe. And, as I now look at what I have written, it seems over-simple; but it's what I know and believe about God and the ways we learn to know him. I am sure of one thing: New insights will change what I know again and again.

I am sure we all know how the learning process works, but let me state it in one way that I know:

1. We acquire knowledge from some source.
2. We try out new behavior based on our new understandings.
3. Having assimilated from this knowledge and experience some things which have meaning for us, we find that these meaningful learnings become a part of who we are.
4. From the change that takes place in who we are may come the motivation to seek new knowledge

and experience, or to wait for these things to come our way.

5. The cycle repeats itself—often, if we are open to change; seldom, if we are closed to change.

Both of the words *Christianity* and *education,* strongly imply change. Change is very costly to an individual. Something new in my life will replace something already there. How do I choose? How do I know something new will be better than the old?

Christianity asks each person not only to make some very large changes, but to believe so totally in an invisible God that we are willing to turn our whole existence over to him, to work for him, to submit to him, to suffer for him, to die for him.

We are told that the physical life is for our use in understanding and developing the spiritual life (the real one). We can choose the physical life at the exclusion of the spiritual if we wish, and live as we choose until we really do die. But, we are urged to choose the spiritual life which goes at least beyond this earthly existence— and perhaps forever.

We are told that turning our power over to God and doing his will gives us rewards of serenity and an amazing amount of assurance and insight.

I am probably in the same place many other people are. From the assimilation of knowledge and experience, I have become intellectually convinced about Christianity. I can also say that I have committed my life to God.

But, I have not *become* what I understand to be a totally Christian person. I am a sinner. When I am in the middle of a doubt, I sometimes turn to God for help, and he helps me. All too often I try to *be* God.

Nevertheless, I am making progress, and I thank God

for that. I also thank countless people, through whom God has been able to reach me, for their faith. How I reached the point I have reached in my faith is very important to me because it helps me to know how to teach. If I am going to be effective as a teacher, I must not only be able to say what I believe, but how that has worked for me in my spiritual growth. People need to hear me say out loud what I believe. And, I need to be ready to back up my beliefs in personal encounters with those who have started to trust me.

After twenty-nine years as a staff person for Christian education, I have returned to a parish. Since I see myself as a full-time teacher of Christianity, and I think that is the role of any rector of any parish, it is my wish to do the best I can as a teacher. I have looked hard at how Christianity is *really* taught and have made some conclusions which now guide me:

1. The best available opportunity I have to teach is in the pulpit. I have said that to my congregation. I speak the truth as I know it from the Gospel. I expect that spoken truth to open minds.
2. The next best opportunity I have to teach is in my pastoral role, one to one, as often as I can, as a pastor, mentor, and spiritual director. And, I have declared this intention to the congregation.
3. Out of these opportunities arise the many other opportunities to teach by creating the very best learning climate, coaching and supporting those who also teach, providing resources—and more. Each of us, whatever our vocation, has our own unique opportunities for teaching about Christianity.

Individuals have to cross over from fear to faith in order to begin a life of study and growth and true ministry. Some of the questions that stop people are about the very things God promises: Everlasting life? Prayer? How can such things be true?

I believe that the bulk of "Christian education" takes place in an unintentional way. It just happens. Some of the lore and myth that is passed on is horribly distorted and misleading to those who honestly seek God. That which comes from the heart of a "true believer" is passed on to others, often without a spoken word. But, in all that we do or say about Christianity and how it is taught, we must remember that God moves in mysterious ways to perform his miracles on our lives—when he chooses. If we are to be God's vehicle for reaching others, we must know that it is sometimes risky, frightening, distasteful, and very hard work. We cannot in the name of God act like God, but only be where he wants us to be so that his will may be done.

13

Between Story and Vision

by NORMA MARRS

As one reflects upon the real thrust of a Christian education approach, what models will work, why in one place and not in another, it prompts me to wonder if we are trying to answer questions that are not being asked. Are we indeed offering what our people think they want, only to find it isn't meeting the real need? "We want a Bible study," they say—then drop out when the content does not satisfy a need they felt would be answered by that study. Perhaps their quest should be for a study that would use the Bible as a resource book to answer some of the basic questions we all have about life: *Who am I? Why am I here in this place and time? What Is God's plan for my life? How can I face fear, anxiety, and even my own death?*

Perhaps if I could simplify a definition of Christian education for those of us who must plan for educational models, it would be this: "Christian education is a process, intentional or unintentional, that moves our people from where they are to what God is calling them to be." Often we are called on to go through personal deserts, wilderness periods, as a means of reaching a promised land, or meaning for our own life.

This definition is short, but not simple! To be involved in moving a person from one place in life to an-

other requires change. It may be from one rut to another, but it is change, nevertheless. It involves changing
thought patterns, arranging priorities to reflect a new
value system, modifying behavior patterns in order to
become a new person in Christ. It requires knowing
where they are in order to help them see where they
should be. Where is their particular spot in the desert and
how far it is to their "promised land?" At what point did
they find themselves living in a desert wilderness—or
what was the genesis of their particular problem?

It is not easy to admit one is in a desert, or looking
hopelessly for a spot to find peace and joy. Our peers
do not take easily to weakness, or loss of direction in us,
as it is often viewed as a sign of failure. It is not easy to
grow old in the middle of a youth-oriented culture,
when you hear a different drumbeat and feel out of step
with everyone else. What may be a desert wilderness for
one is already yesterday's memory for others—and they
may even see a mountaintop ahead.

"Where our people are" may still be in the past, cling-
ing to old securities with change coming too fast to keep
up with it. "Old securities" in the church could be the
old Prayer Book, only men in round collars, the same
service schedule because it has always been done that
way. It may be a guild group that no longer has any
members, but no one is brave enough to let it die and
bring new life in another way.

As for the other end of our Christian education definition, "What is God calling us to be" is a large order as
there is much to be done by the Christian educator. To
develop a "process" as our definition states, involves a
plan of action, an approach to dealing with the status
quo of where we are, to the unknown life and excite-
ment of what he might become with God's help.

I believe God sees us as he created us, whole and holy

persons—a delight to him because he made us. He knows our great potential and sees the good that lives in each of us. He knows our weakness, but what we see as our limitations is not God's vision of and for us. As Paul said, "I can do all things through Christ who strengtheneth me." And Jesus said, "Ask and you shall receive." We ask for power, or love, or strength—and we receive it. But who could not say that God knew that we already had that capacity within us? That God helped us unlock our hidden strengths and helped us find the power that was already there. We have the potential for becoming what we ought to be if we can catch a glimpse of God's vision for us. We see as through a glass darkly, but he knows our whole worth, the person we really are. How else could Christ have been freely offered as a sacrifice for us? As each person recognizes the power or Spirit of God that lives in him, it is released to the extent we can deal with it and let it move us through and beyond our personal deserts. Man was made in God's image—perfect, with capacities that go beyond our understanding. We are God's highest glory and his delight. To deny the Spirit of truth and love that is God-like in us is denying God and his presence.

The church is made up of a group of fellow wanderers, each with his or her own particular spot in the desert. We all have our own unique weakness but we also share to an extent a vision of God, his promise, his protection, and his salvation.

This vision or understanding of God doesn't usually come through a particular Bible story, nor could we recite which chapter and verse changed our life. It more likely comes through reflection on that story, discussion, sharing the story and experience with others until it becomes our own story. There comes a moment in one's reflection when mere facts and data becomes an *aha!* experience. This is explained by Thomas Groome very well in his essay "Shared Christian Praxis": "The Story must be critically remembered so we can transform it in our presents and in freedom create the Vision." If the story is recalled merely to give direction for the present, it is not liberating but merely moving to another rut in the desert to begin all over again. Dr. Groome goes on to say, "The Christian Educator must present the Christian Story and the Vision toward which it points." The story must be retold, time and again for all to hear, know, learn, and somehow reflect and relate it to the vision that God has for us. It is in the telling, sharing, and reflecting that we can see the truth behind the story that has meaning for us.

It would seem that the more adept we are at doing the reflective process and connecting the vision to our story, the easier it will be to *do* the process to bring about a praxis more readily. It would seem that a function of a Christian educator would be to provide opportunities to practice this reflective process, intentionally recalling moments when we first realized we were not living in a perfect world—and that life was really not a big bowl of cherries. There is real sin in the world and if we are honest we know we are part of it—and where did it begin in our life? A simple diagrammatic explanation of this theory appears on page 80.

The more aware I am that I can find answers and feel the presence of God in my life—the sooner I will again seek his guidance. I will turn to him sooner in my desert places rather than suffering through long periods of desolation, as my reflection will bring an awareness that he is already there with me. He has said, "I will not leave you desolate." If I am desolate—it is I who has not looked for God. He is already there and all I have to do is reach out, ask—and I will know that because he lives, I shall live again also. Not in a way I may wish or predict, but in a way that is best for me.

Our Story	**C.E. Process:**	**God's Vision**
(Where we are)	hearing	(What we are called to
in the desert	sharing	be)
pain	remembering	whole
anxiety	offering	holy
problems	destroying	perfect
	building	at-one-with Christ
	shaping	
	loving	
	forgiving	

The more we can *intentionally* and consciously do this process of reflection in a nurturing environment the easier it will be to reach Praxis—or that moment when we understand God's vision and we are moved to action in Christ's name.

If I acknowledge the presence of God in all things and under all circumstances the gap narrows between my story and God's vision for me. It might, in time, become this:

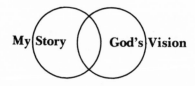

. . . and my life may reflect the presence of God within me. He is already there, as I have said earlier but my *self* gets in the way of acknowledging God as my motivating force. It is he who lifts my life and not me by my own bootstraps. It is he who has led me out of my desert places, and not my own initiative.

It is also, as God is recognized within the community of believers, the church, that we can collectively have our common story become closer to God's vision. If I personally can have my own story and God's vision become one, so can my church learn to work through its common hurts to find God's vision for our common life together. As the Rev. David Perry has so beautifully put it in his article, "Journeying Environment," "The Kingdom of God is here, now, among you . . . our task is not to bring God into the creation—because God is already there . . . the task is to enable persons to discover that God is where they are." This puts a new dimension to my suffering and yours. We are not in it alone. "I will not leave you desolate," could bring comfort to a family that has lost a home in a tornado—or to a person dying of cancer.

The church, made up of collective persons, learning the process of working through the gap between story and vision can be the incarnate Christ to us in our personal pain, and say, "We are all learning to share, love, forgive, cry, care, and we want to surround you with our love. Because you are part of us and we of you—we want you to know God loves you and we are all hanging in there with you."

It doesn't take a structured program or curricula to go to someone's side and help them through the desert. It is God's vision that this is what we should become— his hands and feet in the world. While text books and classes may teach one how to deal with crises, there is special grace given to anyone who simply wants to be present, to say, "I am here I care about what happens to you."

There is no curriculum that can teach *thoroughly* and deeply about Christian love until the participants have put the book aside, reflected, and then put their love to work.

It is probably through *unintentional* education that we are the best teachers. It is by *being, doing,* the way we handle our own stories, our own desert experiences, the way we affirm the presence of God, the way we respond and worship him that we are really teaching the faith. It is how we accept the unlovely, and forgive the sinner, that we teach about Jesus' way. Our children learn of true Christian love by the way we all live it out together.

As a Christian educator I like to plan events that will let the unexpected happen—to be an enabler to let the "family" gather on every occasion possible to celebrate our "togetherness," from a coffee hour to a corporate communion and breakfast. I believe it is in these shared experiences that we learn to know each other better, miss the absent, worry about the ill, care for the older people, laugh and play with the babies, welcome the college students home, celebrate birthdays, holidays. Those are the memories our children will reflect on when they are in their own desert places—and they will remember not only the love we gave them, but that we had shared a vision of what it means to be a child of God; loved, accepted, and affirmed.

One of the greatest things we can aim for in Christian education, intentionally or unintentionally, is providing a nurturing environment where we can grow and recognize the presence of Christ in each of us. To help make our personal story of who we are closer to the reality of what God wants us to become. Our people are really saying, *"Help us find meaning in our lives in the midst of where we are." "Where is God?" "If Christ lives, help me find him from within my desert." "How can I lose the fear of growing old?" "Help me face up to the reality of tomorrow morning." "How can I survive in this competitive world?" "What is the point of trying to be good?" "Who cares?"* I believe that these are the concerns and questions in the hearts of our people, and they are the real questions we have to deal with in a theology for Christian education.

As we answer these questions we will, both intentionally and unintentionally, teach the great truths of salvation history—God's own story as he has revealed himself in the lives of his people, and continues to reveal his mighty acts. It is as we reflect on his intervention into the life of humans that we recognize and accept his vision as a viable and necessary way of life for us.

14

Transformation and Growth

by JAMES H. OTTLEY

Christian education is the process through which the individual is confronted with the life of Christ; his life is transformed and he continues to grow by his daily experiences with Christ and to other humans. And as a result of this transformation he then proceeds to offer his life in worship to God and service to others.

Christian education so understood is not something that takes place at one stage of our lives, but is rather a continuous process which is active at every stage of our development.

Christian education, although it may provide some answers, should also provoke man to seek response as to his existence as a child of God and to determine his responsibilities to God, himself, and the people of God.

Christian education must take into consideration the time in which we live, the culture where it is being expressed and as dynamic force discover with others the Good News of the Gospel.

The curriculum of Christian education is life. All of life and not a segment of it. It is not something that happens once a week or during infancy and school age, but rather it is our continuous awareness of who we are and how we can best offer to God the life he has entrusted to us.

Christian education is, first, man's response to Christ's, "Come unto him, to follow him." It is, further, our response to his command to go into the world "baptizing and teaching." As we respond in this way, *we offer*. It is this offering which magnifies the dynamic process as we continuously seek to respond and to offer. This two-fold process gives meaning to life as we seek to know Christ and make him known. To teach, then, is to learn and to learn is to teach. In this way, teachers and students are locked together in their constant search to know Christ and to make known.

One of the tasks of Christian education is to bring us to the realization that all of our actions in our daily life are of equal importance to God, and that these, therefore, are opportunities for learning. To make Christian education anything less is to relegate it to secondary position in our lives and rob it of its significance. The changing world in which we live today demands that we be dynamic in our approach to education, enabling man, within the bonds of freedom, to be creative in his effort to serve God and his fellow humans. Christian education equips us for service and for sacrifice, and makes real our responsibility to love God and our neighbor as ourselves.

15

Working Together

by NANCY RAYFIELD

First of all, as an artist, I see Christian education as green—the color of living, growing things. It is every shade, from a cool, deep, conservative forest green to a wild and exciting chartreuse. One finds green every-where, in the sea and in the mountains, in a loved one's eyes, or even on moldy orange peels in a gutter. This is the intuitive part of Christian education.

It is real and valid, but Christian education is also in-tellectual, and has words as well as color. St. Paul uncon-sciously defined for me the form and the goal of Chris-tian education in one phrase: "Working together to build up the body of Christ." That is our crucial task. Taken separately out of context what do each of the words imply?

Working
There is something continuing, in process, not static. It moves, with active participation. It takes effort, takes en-ergy, is intentional and not drifting unconsciously. Work implies something productive, results in some change. It is useful; it works!

Together
This says to me Christian education is relationships of interdependence, not something done alone. There is

necessity for corporate action rather than something done *to* or only *for* another. (On the other hand we *can* learn and discover some things alone; religious reflection can be done alone; I alone am responsible for my own learning.) But "together" implies elements of separate identity. God finds each of us unique and valuable to him!

Build Up

Here are implications of being creative and constructive. We are called to be co-creators with God. Christian education grows and discloses new horizons at every step forward. At the same time there must be a foundation for support. I think there are certain basics: Attitudes (feelings which influence our behavior); skills (lots of "how-to's" for what we do); Knowledge (information we gain—and forget—and respond to). Put them together and get A.S.K. Christian education is built on asking the right questions of yourself, of teachers, of God.

Body of Christ

This phrase carries with it more images and similes than are found in the other words. "Body of Christ" reveals that Christian education is unlimited, not exclusively for any group, or any time of life. It works in, through, and for, the sake of Christian community. Christ is the great educator from whom we discover what it means to be Christian.

Elsewhere, St. Paul speaks of our gifts of ministry, "some are called to teach." On the contrary, I understand teaching as something we *all* are called to do and are doing. We teach by our lives, as we minister to each other. We can't help it—although I admit some teach more intentionally than others!

The details of organization and techniques of Christian education are infinite; the content is as broad as all our concerns; but the purpose is single: working together to build up the Body of Christ—in living color. Thanks be to God!

16

Coming to Faith

by DOROTHY M. WATT

"Follow me!" This injunction of Jesus' is quoted six times in the Gospel of Matthew alone. Centuries later Christians are still striving to obey that command. Just two simple words but such a difficult task when we study the example lived for us by Christ.

One example set for us by Jesus was his ability as a master teacher who had many skills at his command but who taught each person in terms related to the life and needs of that person whether someone in the crowd of followers, one of the twelve disciples, or a Pharisee. As followers of Jesus, each of us must teach by the life we live, the faith we share, or by helping others to learn in more formal ways. To be teachers we must also be learners.

Christian education is the process by which we learn and teach in the church. It is a life-long process which takes place not only in the church building but wherever Christians find hemselves. Without the educational process, the church could die with this generation.

If the Christian faith is to be transmitted from generation to generation, Christian education must be a function of the total life of the church. In the 20th century, Christian education became a department of the church, focused on formal classes about the faith. There is much to be taught formally about the Christian faith and its source book, the Bible. However if the church delegates to a small group of people the responsibility for all education, the Christian faith is in danger of becoming a cold and lifeless set of facts *about* a faith.

In times past, a child grew up in a family with Christ as the center of the household and prayer as a natural part of family life. The child was nourished by faith as by food and love. More often than not, the child also went to a school where most of the other children were growing up in the same faith and had similar moral values. For many of today's children, neither assumption can be made. Religion has been banned from the public schools, and parents who grew up in that sheltered environment with an unquestioning acceptance of the faith of others are no longer confident enough of their own faith to share it with their children (or worse yet have come to believe that only special people are able to teach their children).

Today's schools reflect the mobility of our present society and contain a microcosm of the society which they serve. Children with varied beliefs and ways of expressing those beliefs as well as children with no religious faith or those who are openly hostile to religion now share the same classrooms. The Christian child needs tools to help him explain his understandings of the Christian faith and to help him act in Christian ways when peers try to lead in other paths. The church must find effective ways in which to help both children and adults be personally committed to their faith and to continue to grow and mature in that faith.

In God's Old Covenant with humankind, he asked his covenant people to remain separate from the worshippers of other gods. Christ brought us a New Covenant and said, "Go into all the world and preach the Gospel"

(Mark 16:15). This New Covenant was preached to Jew and gentile, but Christians still maintained their separation from those with other beliefs. Early in the 20th century, in this country, Christians separated themselves from non-Christians. Even groups within the Christian community maintained their separate areas with their own church in the center.

Now our mobile society with its mass communication has forced us into going into all the world to preach and live the Gospel, and to recognize that Christians are a minority in a secular world. Christian education must be carried out intentionally in the total life of the Christian community without expecting support from the school or the secular world. Few Christians today are able to meet the demands and challenges of their adult life with the faith acquired as a child. Instead of censuring those who question what they've learned, the church must see the questioning and searching member as a growing and maturing person. Instead of crying "heretic" and turning away, the church must provide settings in which answers may be sought and new questions asked. The true Christian answers, "I believe" and not, "the church says." With maturity, the ending to the "I believe" sentence will change as the Christian discovers ever deeper and broader concepts of Christianity both through experience and through study.

Christian education, then, is that life-long process through which faith is acquired, deepened, and made one's own. Christian education has the dual role of conveying information about the Christian faith and at the same time providing settings in which faith can be explored and deepened with mentors to help develop insights and attitudes about faith experiences. Christian education may be responsible for providing some programs, but even more it is a dimension of the total life of the Christian community and a perspective on that community.

In Corinthians 12:28, Paul lists teachers as the third group appointed by God, just after apostles and prophets. The professional Christian educators are those specially trained persons, both lay and ordained, who intentionally use life situations for faith development and for cognitive learning about Christianity. These educators must have a strong and maturing faith of their own and a desire to share it. They also need an understanding of the different modes through which people acquire knowledge, and an understanding of age level differences in learning styles and subjects, and especially they must be aware of individual differences and concerns in any learning situation.

There are many learning tools available to Christian education from public education, the behavioral sciences, human development studies, and the counseling field. An effective educator makes appropriate use of all of these tools in planning a long-range, total program for a Christian community. While the Christian educator may have expertise in one or more areas, it is more important to be a generalist who is able to see a total program, to know when a specialist in method or content should be called, and to have the resources to locate a suitable expert.

The Christian educator should also be an observer of the whole life of the community and a question asker. Leaders of other programs should be asked what they see as the educational dimension of the programs they lead and offered help in choosing the most effective means of accomplishing that purpose whether it is to build fellowship, share faith experiences, or study a Bible passage. Questions could be asked about what is being taught by the usual way of doing the liturgy and what might be taught by occasional changes in such things as readers, presentation of gifts, etc. Questions should even be asked as to what the building itself teaches about welcoming newcomers, concern for the handicapped, the importance of children and youth, and many other aspects of the Christian faith.

While the specially-trained Christian educator, lay or clergy, has a leadership and administrative role to play in Christian education, the most important teaching is done by parents, the dedicated teachers, retreat leaders, camp counselors, and others. This teaching is done by both word and deed, formally and informally. We must remember that each member of a congregation is a minister and disciple of Christ and teaches by the life lived every day, by the services given to those who touch that life, by the love expressed through words or actions which tell the world what the Good News really means. These ministers are the teachers in the office, factory, committee meeting, classroom, playground, hospital, highway, and all the places to which life takes them. These ministers have the greatest opportunity to express Christ to the non-Christian and to call the un-churched back to their faith. If these sound like evan-gelistic or mission activities, it is because the ministry of the church cannot be segmented. It must be integrated in a wholistic approach. Education has a place in each activity of the church, and each part of ministry (liturgy, mission, evangelism, discipleship, etc.) must have a place in education.

These lay ministers of the church must be empowered by the church, helped to recognize their role as teachers, and helped to realize that "not to each is to teach." They need and expect from the church continuing help in heightening their awareness of what they *are* teaching, of what Christ would *ask* them to teach, and help in attaining a closer personal relationship with Christ and their Creator.

The ultimate Christian education happens when the human soul finds itself barefoot on holy ground in the awesome presence of the Creator, Almighty God.

17

Between Fact and the Christ Event in Life

by LADONNA M. WIND

As I reflect upon the theology of Christian education, I get caught up in my feeble effort to understand the good works and good words of my Lord, Jesus Christ. The Christ event has a richness that offers me a lifelong journey toward a deeper understanding and acceptance of who I am, and who I am in relationship to God. I must ask the question, "Will I ever totally understand?" If I can't, how then can I ever, as an educator, lead others to an understanding? How do I envision the Christ? What do I see in life that points to the Cross, to the Resurrection, and to my life lived in and through him? As I struggle, sometimes the questions become more complex. But then I finally understand that I am about a process that will ultimately take me beyond myself. I will somehow overcome my own limitations. I will be able to approach the good works and involve myself in them, and I will be able to hear and understand the good words, the Good News, the Gospel of my Lord, Jesus Christ.

If this, then, is a lifelong journey—a process that begins early and proceeds throughout my life—what does this say to the church about our educational process? It says to me, that I need total understanding about the

Christian life. It says I need information about this man called Jesus. It says I need an understanding or knowledge of history in order to make some sense out of life—its pain and sorrow, its joy and rejoicing. But it also says to me that I need to know the event. And I can only *know* that in my heart. How then, does this knowing occur? For me, it is in working toward a theology of Christian education—learning the fact, experiencing the Christ event, and acting it out in my life. Let the educational process begin!

In order to be in process of becoming the person God calls me to be, I must understand the historical Christ. He did walk this earth. He did teach. He did suffer. He did die. He did rise again and ascend into Heaven. He did the impossible. He overcame that which we, in our limitations, find difficult to understand. But through him we can understand. The factual Christ becomes a reality for us through the good words he shared with the people among whom he walked. Reading as we do the accounts of our Lord's life as shared through Scripture, we "see" Jesus among the people. He taught about the Father; he taught a new meaning of Scripture; he taught love of humankind by being among the people who were cast aside, who were shunned, and who were despised. He taught by saying things in a different way, by challenging people to think and reflect. He taught by being available to the people. He taught by living the life God called him to live. He taught by being an example that all would be called to follow. Jesus invested all of himself in life. As we delve more deeply into the meaning behind those words and the good works he did, we come to know a man who was human. He felt pain and disappointment. He felt failure just as we do. He questioned and got angry. He felt human emotion just as we do. This must be part of what the church teaches its people about Jesus. We must first of all understand his humanness, and then we can come to understand him as having transcended all that is human. It is a process that must begin from the very beginning of our life lived in the worshipping community.

When we begin to understand the historical Christ, then we can begin to better understand the Christ event. It is at this point that we begin to become total persons. We are in the process of working toward something— the Christian event, the total freedom that breaks the chains of uncertainty about what we are and where we are going. We know that the Christ event offers more. We move from the childhood of faith into the maturity of life in Christ. And we know that we are part of the ongoing community, the communion of saints that have gone before, and the present living community of people. We have a new feeling, a new vision, a new meaning for life. We have crossed from the historical Christ to the Christ event.

To know the Christ event and freedom it offers, I must take the knowledge learned by study and prayer and reflect upon it. When I pray, even the simple prayer of a child, I open myself to conversation with God. It is through these conversations that I come to experience Christ. By living a prayer centered life, I am changed daily into being the person I am meant to be. The pain of today is shared in my quiet, private talks with God, and I am blessed and enriched with his grace to overcome, to survive, to accept, and to move on. I come to understand in my heart and mind that God does listen, he does care, he does sustain. And the more conversations I have with him, the better able I am to know the Christ event. These, then, are experiences that I am hard pressed to put into words, but I can share by the third step in my theology of Christian education, and that is action.

The educational process must be seen as that lifelong journey that we take with Christ. It is sharing the story of where Jesus is in life with me. It must not be seen as achieving something in my lifetime. It must not be just for preparing me for receiving the sacraments and nothing more. The stages in the educational process must not be treated as stepping stones to be achieved one after the other like winning prizes at the county fair. But instead the educational process must enable me to experience the ongoingness of growth as a Christian. I must enjoy the process—it must have a special dynamic all of its own. The process needs to be that which helps me to answer the *how* of my relationship with God. It is that process that helps me as a Christian reflect upon my life lived in and through Jesus, no matter how successfully or unsuccessfully that life has been lived. He helps me, by reflection, to see God acting in my life. I see his good works and I am called into good works also. He provides me with unlimited actions to be involved in. I need only ask for direction and he will lead.

God's created world is filled with opportunities to act—or to refrain from acting. These need not be grandiose, large-scale actions; they may be simple daily acts of kindness. We can lead others to see God's world as he created it and appreciate its beauty, observe its simpleness and complexity and preserve what we see for someone else who will come after us. The simple decision *not* to litter; the act of pointing out to a friend a hummingbird, a pretty flower, squirrels scampering about or sharing any number of things in nature is an act of sharing. Reaching out and shaking someone's hand, patting them on the shoulder, hugging them, smiling at them, listening to them is an act of acceptance and acknowledgment of their worth. As we grow in understanding, taking on tasks of helping others is an act of love. The actions we are called to by our knowledge of Jesus and our conversations through prayer with him, will be all those things from the everydayness of life. I hear his good words and I am beckoned to study those good words. Therefore, my journey is a journey of sought for knowledge, experiences of the heart learned through prayer and living out the Christ event which gives me freedom to be.

God calls me to a fulltime commitment and I answer passionately and with no regret or apology. He calls me to continue to act through and in light of the Good News. I join the throngs of fellow faith-travelers along the road of discovery. It is to be filled with only those things that the Event makes possible.

In preparation for teaching the facts, the church must again stress the importance of the basic facts. The richness of our heritage is shared with us as it marches across the pages of the Bible. Here is the story of God's continuing to work at being a companion to his people throughout the ages. We are part of that story and must see ourselves in it. It must come alive to us. This is the story of the reality of the world. God's people were taught to pray and we too must pray as Jesus taught, "Our Father who art in heaven . . ." (Matt. 6:9–15) He speaks to us individually in the quiet solitude of our hearts and minds during our private prayer when he says, "My sheep hear my voice and I know them and they follow me."

I believe the church is called to once again help us to see our relationship with Christ as being a daily effort. It is not reserved just for Sundays and Sunday school classes. But rather it is the daily effort to stay alive in the world. The greatest way to teach is by example. What kind of lives do we live? What kind of examples do we use? What do we show to the world? Where are our priorities? What are our values?

Our educational process must be planned and un-planned, felt and observed, doing and becoming. It is not so much the words that we say, but the actions un-derscoring those words. My task then, as an educator, and, I believe, the task of the church, is to redeem and to salvage, nurture not alienate, soothe not create dis-harmony, accept not reject, reach out and give not only receive, recognize but not expect recognition. There-fore, I see Christian education in this model:

History	**Event**	**Action**
(knowledge of the head)	(experience of the heart)	(sharing the experience)

which occurs through:

> *Sacraments, sacrifice, understanding, acceptance, action, reaction, working, giving, being, doing, and love.*

which then leads to:

> *wholeness that is incarnational, redemptive, present, and future.*

Perhaps, then, we as Christian educators, we as students, and we as fellow seekers after truth will see ourselves as God sees us:

> So God created man in his own image, in the image of God he created him; male and female he created them . . . and God saw everything that he had made and behold it was very good.
>
> *Genesis 1:27–30*)

An Afterword

You've been hearing about other peoples' theology and its implication for the ministry of Christian education. Now you might wish to write your own theology. Here are some suggestions about how to do it.

Begin by identifying the key elements of your faith and belief. These questions may help you do that:

· How does God speak to you?
· How is God revealed to you?
· Who are the people who have given meaning to your life?
· What are the events that have had the most meaning in your life?
· What have you learned from these people and events?
· What Biblical stories remind you of yourself?
· In what ways are you like David or Abraham or Rebekah or Judas or Mary or Jesus—or whatever figure from the Bible in whom you find something of yourself?
· What in the tradition of the church means the most to you? What creed (if any)?
· What aspects of church tradition or of the creeds has given you problems?
· Focus on a problem or critical issue in your life and form a statement of belief about it.
· What affirmations of faith can you make?

· How can you share your faith and belief with another person?
· How are you called to do and be God's worth?
· How are we to respond?
· How do you define Christian education? What are your goals for Christian education?
· What methods and philosophies of teaching and learning are consistent with the theology which you have named and spoken?

You may find it helpful to write down your reflections in the blank pages provided at the end of this book.

If theology can be seen as making sense of things, then perhaps our task as Christian educators is to become more conscious of that reality. Perhaps our approaches and methods in religious education could—and should—reflect more closely in actions that which we affirm theologically in our thoughts and words. And we can focus our efforts on doing and living our theology as Christians. Since people understand, as we have said, by stories and signs, perhaps Christian educators should learn to focus on how the images, symbols, and truths of our Christian faith are present in our lives.

Our theologies grow from our actions and reflections. This means that Christian educators might well be more concerned with how we live rather than with what we *know* in a classroom sense. With considerable wisdom, the great German theologian Karl Rahner has said:

> The theological problem today is to find the art of drawing religion out of man, not pumping it into him. The redemption has happened. The Holy Spirit is in Man. The art is to help men become what they are.

David W. Perry

My Own Theology

_____

_____

_____

_____

_____

_____

_____

_____

_____

_____

_____

_____

_____

_____

_____

_____

_____

_____

_____